SUZUKI SJ

LJ, SJ410, SJ413
SAMURAI & SANTANA

SUZUKI SJ

LJ, SJ410, SJ413
SAMURAI & SANTANA

THE ENTHUSIAST'S COMPANION

EDITOR: RAY HUTTON

MRP

MOTOR RACING PUBLICATIONS LTD
Unit 6, The Pilton Estate, 46 Pitlake, Croydon CR0 3RY, England.

First Published 1989

British Library Cataloguing in Publication Data
Suzuki SJ.
   1. Suzuki. Cars.
   I.   Hutton, Ray
   629.2

ISBN 0 947981 34 9

Photoset by Tek-Art Ltd, West Wickham, Kent
Printed in Great Britain by
The Amadeus Press Ltd
Huddersfield, West Yorkshire

CONTENTS

INTRODUCTION

Not many vehicles can claim as wide an appeal as the four-wheel-drive Suzukis. Country folk use them as light but versatile workhorses. Those who live in places rendered inaccesible by winter weather have them as a lifeline. Yet young city-dwellers have taken to them as a new kind of sports car, cheap to buy, economical to run, and a lot more fun than a conventional small car.

Over 10 years on the UK market, starting with the spartan, utilitarian LJ and moving up to the latest gaily-painted SJs, the little Suzukis have gained a lot of friends. Many have been encouraged by the vehicles' go-anywhere ability to try off-road driving for the first time, and even take part in competitive trials.

Most Suzuki 4x4 owners are enthusiasts. Not, perhaps, in the same sense as those who follow motor racing and rallying and glory in exotic high performance cars, but enthusiasts for their own special kind of motoring. This book is for them.

It is intended for everyone who owns, or would like to own, a Suzuki 4x4. It begins with the fascinating background to the LJ and SJ series, the versions sold around the world, and the hows and whys of their construction. It goes on to provide practical advice on maintenance, the selection of accessories, and what to look for when buying a vehicle secondhand.

Expert authors with broad experience of four-wheel drive vehicles were asked to provide a critical analysis of the current SJ design and its on and off-road performance. They pull no punches about the disadvantages as well as the advantages of these low-cost vehicles that, inevitably, have to compromise between the very different requirements of on- and off-road motoring.

Aware that most owners will have graduated to an SJ from a conventional road car, we conclude with chapters on off-road driving for leisure and sport. Experienced 4x4 drivers will find some of this familiar stuff, but we hope they will agree that constant re-emphasizing the safe, legal and socially acceptable way to use off-road vehicles is necessary to allow this pleasurable pursuit to continue on these crowded islands. For those who have caught the off-road bug there is a chapter on appropriate clubs and various levels of competition, from trials for unmodified road vehicles to more serious international events.

This is an unusual book because it deals with an unusual vehicle. Its advice and information is not deeply technical but neither is it shallow. It is designed to be practical and to entertain – just like the Suzuki SJ. Whatever form your enthusiasm takes, it should enable you to get more out of your four-wheel drive Suzuki. That's why it is called The Enthusiast's Companion.

Social climber

How a little utility vehicle grew up to become a cult. Ray Hutton traces the evolution of Suzuki's practical-but-fun 4x4s

RAY HUTTON writes about cars and the motor business for the *Sunday Express Magazine, Punch,* and a number of trade and industry publications in the UK, as well as the top American magazine *Car and Driver.* A former Editor of *Autocar,* Ray is also the editor of this MRP Enthusiast's Companion.

When a little truck called the Jimny 360 went on sale in Japan in April 1970 no-one imagined that 10 years later its successor would thrive not only among the rural communities of Japan but on the streets of the world's greatest cities and the playgrounds of the prosperous.

Suzuki were already world-famous for their motorcycles. They made cars too, tiny ones for what was the major part of the Japanese domestic market at the time. The 360cc two-stroke Suzulight was Suzuki's first four-wheeler, unveiled back in 1955. By 1967 the Fronte 360 saloon was established as a best-seller. Its engine was adopted for the Jimny, the company's first venture into the four-wheel drive market.

Why, just as Japanese car makers were turning to more sophisticated products, did Suzuki go back to basics, and build a vehicle for off-road use? Yoshio Saito, Suzuki managing director responsible for automobile overseas operations, explains: 'Suzuki is unusual among automobile companies. We started as a mini-car manufacturer and wanted to meet the need for any kind of miniature vehicle – passenger car, commercial, even four-wheel drive. That

The origins of the Suzuki 4x4 range are in the Hope Star ON360 which was briefly on the Japanese market in 1968 before Suzuki took it over. Their adaptation was the Jimny 360 (LJ10), below, launched in Japan in April 1970. This first LJ had zip-up canvas doors and mounted the spare wheel behind the passenger seat; maximum seating capacity was three.

LJ80 variations. On the left-hand side are the two models first sold in the UK – the 'full convertible' with a simple restraining bar instead of doors and a high padded roll-over bar, and the LJ80V hardtop van. The metal-door soft-top, top right, came a few months later. The LJ81K pick-up, lower right, was an export-only model but was not sold in Britain.

– the 4x4 – was developed for industrial use, where there was a need for a working vehicle that could travel off-road and perhaps in snow. At that time we concentrated on the domestic market and we intended the Jimny for practical use, not so much for fun. That came later!'

The Jimny 360 (which Suzuki code-named LJ10) was essentially a scaled-down version of the American Jeep. Its direct ancestor was, in fact, a long-forgotten four-wheel drive utility called the Hope Star ON360. The now-defunct Hope Motor Company started to develop a 4x4 mini-truck in 1965. It was a very basic vehicle with no doors, fold-down windscreen and hammock seats and it used a Mitsubishi air-cooled two-stroke engine. Only a handful were sold before the Hope company ran into difficulties and in 1968 Suzuki acquired the production rights of the ON360. The Hope Star set the pattern for the Jimny 360 but, naturally, Suzuki substituted their own engine, as well as redesigning many of the vehicle's components.

The size, in any case, was determined by the Japanese 'micro-car' regulations which then allowed a maximum overall length of 3,000mm (118in) and width of 1,300mm (51in). The twin-cylinder engine developed just 25bhp, but since the original Jimny weighed only 600kg (1,322lb), it was not as desperately slow as one might imagine. But performance that was acceptable to a Japanese public weaned on micro-cars was unlikely to be adequate overseas. Before Suzuki's mini-jeep was exported it would require – and would get – a bigger and more powerful engine.

In the early 1970s the demand from developing countries for rugged off-road vehicles was very high. Land Rover, who really invented the 'civilian' jeep just after the Second World War, did not have the capacity to meet all the potential orders. Already, Toyota, Japan's biggest vehicle manufacturer, had launched the Land Cruiser into hungry South-East Asian and African markets. Nissan, Daihatsu, Mitsubishi and other Japanese car makers were waiting in the wings.

In retrospect, this was the time when Land Rover should have been thinking of new products and diversification, but they were too busy making the same old vehicle – and launching the up-market Range Rover. They had turned down the Austin Ant, a Mini-based four-wheel drive utility that had been designed for military use. The parent company British Leyland also stopped UK production of the Mini Moke, the Ant's predecessor, in 1968. The Moke was in many ways the 1960s equivalent of the Suzuki SJ and, had the Ant lived, today's favourite low-cost recreational 4x4 might have been British instead of Japanese.

That the little Suzukis became fashionable fun cars, as well as practical, go-anywhere machines, is largely through the efforts of the British importers. Suzuki had started exporting the LJ to Australia quite early in its career and experience there confirmed that more power was needed. An air-cooled engine was also not the most appropriate for a hard-working vehicle. So there was a change to a water-cooled unit, as first used in Suzuki's little van, then to a three-cylinder 550cc two-stroke, and finally to a conventional four-cylinder, four-stroke of 797cc. It was in this LJ80 form that the vehicle was introduced to the UK.

In 1978, the Heron Corporation, who already imported motorcycles through Heron Suzuki GB Ltd, set up a new company called Suzuki GB (Cars) Ltd to market their four-wheel drive and light commercial vehicles. John Norman, now chief executive of Heron Suzuki GB Ltd, had been responsible for launching Honda cars in Britain in the mid-1960s. Introducing Suzuki four-wheelers, when the dealer network was made up of motorbike specialists, was a similar proposition. But Norman saw a new opportunity with the Suzuki 4x4s. 'We were able to create an entirely new sector of the market,' he remembers. 'There was nothing else in the world that offered four-wheel drive in a light, simple vehicle with an engine of less than 1.6 litres.'

'We set ourselves a five-year objective of positioning the vehicle. We knew we had a price advantage over other 4x4s, but we set out first of all to show that it could do its job, and then gradually to change its image. Market research had shown that the time was right for a well-priced versatile vehicle such as this to be promoted for leisure as well as practical purposes.'

Suzuki's Australian sortie had shown that, too. There, people, both young and old, had already taken to the open-topped LJ80 as a more capable alternative to the beach buggy. The Japanese were mystified by the way that their serious little commerical vehicle was being used, but they trusted the judgment of their importers — and, of course, in time, the Japanese youth market also came to realize that a Suzuki 4x4 could mean motoring fun.

Part of the UK company's carefully laid plan was to make a few LJ80s available to potential customers before launch. Farmers, foresters, shepherds and gamekeepers used the vehicle for their regular country activities and testified to its abilities. The fact that the Suzuki was small was a positive advantage for some of these 'guinea pigs' as the highly manoeuvrable SJ was able to cope with tracks and paths that defeated larger four-wheel drive vehicles. Those included the Land Rover, which had grown over the years. More than one commentator noted that the new Suzuki was of similar size to the original version of the British 4x4 pioneer.

Suzuki GB's first advertisements following the LJ launch on March 29, 1979, emphasized the utility aspects, the four-wheel drive and the high ground clearance. A year later there was a shift of emphasis. The adverts were headlined 'Wild Weekender' and showed an obviously town couple negotiating a muddy slope. 'You can say goodbye to tame weekends', ran the copy line. A follow-up promised that the Suzuki would 'get you out of the jungle' — the urban one, that was.

Nowadays, as Suzuki GB marketing director Ian Catford explains, there is a dual approach. In the winter, advertisements emphasize the hardtop models and the ability to keep going in adverse weather conditions. In the summer the focus is on the great outdoors, the Suzuki's ability to 'get away from it all — and go where others daren't'. In both cases, it is made clear that the Suzuki is a practical all-round, multi-purpose vehicle.

For all their clever marketing, the original LJ80 was a pretty uncivilized device. One review said that it was for masochists only, and that it had 'all the disadvantages of a wartime jeep without the advantages'. That, however, reckoned without the low price (£2,900 in April 1979) and low running costs (30 miles per gallon or more in all kinds of conditions).

With a success on their hands — 'from the start, the four-wheel drive vehicles sold better than we had expected,' says managing director Yoshio Saito —

The start of a new trend – a year after the LJ80 had been established in the UK as a working vehicle, Suzuki GB began to promote the recreational possibilities of this mini 4x4. Adverts like this fitted perfectly with the early-1980s enthusiasm for country matters and outside activities.

Suzuki started to work on developments of the theme. Apart from the bigger engines for export LJs, they had progressed from canvas, zip-up doors to corrugated steel pressings and there were several variations of open and closed bodywork. By 1980 it was time for a completely new model. The SJ series received a new chassis frame, new axles and, for export, a new engine of 970cc. Compared with the LJ, it was longer and wider and sat on a 4in longer wheelbase. The body was restyled with the now-familiar squared-up bonnet with its wider grille and more elaborate bumpers.

In Japan the basic model continued with a 550cc engine, complying with the (revised and slightly enlarged) micro-car regulations. By 1982 the domestic-market Jimny SJ30 was joined by the 1000 SJ410 – the vehicle that we have today as the Santana.

Having expanded vehicle production dramatically over a decade, Japanese manufacturers were becoming acutely aware of trade pressures all over the world. In Britain a 'gentlemen's agreement' between the British and Japanese industries limiting Japanese cars to 11% of the market has been in operation since 1975. Similar quota agreements apply to 4x4s and commercial vehicles. Latecomers like Suzuki have only a small allocation and are unable to expand with Japan-built products. Faced with similar difficulties if they wanted to sell in the United States, Suzuki began to investigate overseas production.

The first step in America was to make a marketing agreement with General Motors which would introduce Suzuki products wearing Chevrolet badges. Suzuki and GM then agreed to set up a joint-venture assembly plant in Canada.

In Europe, Suzuki were more interested in expanding 4x4 and commercial vehicle sales. The Spanish company Land Rover Santana SA were looking for a product to complement their licence-built Land Rovers. The companies were a good fit and they made a technical agreement in 1982 which would lead to Spanish production of the SJ410. By then Suzuki had taken a 20% (later increased to 32%) shareholding in Santana (in which Land Rover now have a 23% stake). The 20,000 SJ410s now built each year at their Linares plant in

Arrival of the SJ Series – Suzuki GB leave no doubt about the image they seek to create with the SJ410Q soft-top, left, while the metal top is presented with rear-side windows as a passenger vehicle, centre, and as the SJ410V commercial.

Practical application – SJ410QB is the commercial soft-top identical to the passenger version except for its lack of rear seats and windows in the hood sides.

southern Spain have over 60% local content and so qualify as European under Common Market rules and are therefore not part of Suzuki GB's quota.

In 10 years Suzuki have progressed from being a rather insular car maker focussed on the Japanese home market to a world player selling in more than 100 countries and assembling vehicles as far afield as India, Pakistan and Indonesia. Suzuki GB now receives supplies from three sources – Japan, Spain and Luton, in Bedfordshire, where the little Supercarry van is made alongside the Bedford Rascal in the IBC joint-venture commercial vehicle operation.

Because of their success in positioning the 4x4 as a multi-purpose vehicle, Suzuki GB became closely involved in the development of the SJ410 and, particularly, deciding how the Santana version should be specified. In conjunction with their counterparts in Europe, they encouraged the use of softer springs for a more comfortable on-road ride and the provision of a five-speed gearbox (though the four-speed remained standard for Santanas sold in Spain). They also helped devise a range of bright colour schemes and graphics, some of which remained exclusive to British market models, like the all-white Santana, the all-black Santana Sport and the hardtop SJ410VX.

The Santana models became available in the UK in the spring of 1987. Spain became the source for all SJ410s sold here, while the vehicles brought in from Japan were of the new SJ413 series, using the 1.3-litre engine of the Suzuki Swift saloon.

The SJ413, with its up-rated interior, 2.75in wider track and extended wheelarches, was first exported to Canada. It was sold there as the Suzuki Samurai and entered the US market as that early in 1986. This was the first time that Suzuki had sold cars in the United States under its own name (though the Swift had been marketed as the Chevrolet Sprint some time before).

The Samurai had a good reception from the American press. *Car and Driver* were intrigued by what they called 'a pint-sized four-wheel drive truck'. Their first road test concluded: 'What we have here is your basic cheap Jeep. If you want a rugged four-wheel driver for the minimum amount of money, the Samurai is the only game in town. Our advice to Suzuki is to crank up the assembly plants and send Samurais by the boatload. A hungry market awaits.'

Sure enough, the SJ gained a lot of young friends in the land that invented the hot-rod and the beach buggy. Its popularity was such that it drew the attention of the busy-body consumer organizations which the United States has in profusion.

In June 1988, the Consumers Union, publishers of *Consumer Reports* magazine, alleged that their tests showed that the Samurai had an alarming tendency to roll over when cornering. Using this information, the Washington-based Center for Auto Safety, called on the US government's NHTSA (National Highway and Traffic Safety Administration) to re-call all Samurais sold in the US since 1986 for safety modifications.

Taking a lead from the Consumers Union, Britain's Consumers' Association drew attention to what they called 'the serious public safety hazard' presented by the Suzuki SJ's instability in the July 1988 edition of *Which?* They said that sales of the Suzuki SJ should be stopped.

The Minister for Roads and Traffic, Peter Bottomley, responded by setting up an independent investigation through the Transport Road Research Laboratory.

Serious motoring writers came to the SJ's defence, questioning the relevance of these tests to everyday driving, and pointing out what was surely obvious to all 4x4 owners and drivers, that a high-set vehicle on multi-purpose tyres cannot be expected to handle like a low-slung modern car and should be driven accordingly. Confident of the safety of their products, Suzuki GB called the CA's allegations 'misleading and discriminating'. Dealers were certainly suffering in sales, as potential buyers were, understandably, alarmed and confused by the controversy.

For once, the government departments on both sides of the Atlantic acted with commendable speed. In September, NHTSA rejected the request for a recall after examining US accident statistics and finding that the Suzuki's

Many SJs have a real country living and are a boon to their owners when there is a sudden snap of winter weather. This one was even able to get out ahead of the snow plough.

record was no worse than for comparable vehicles of other makes. Later that month, the British Department of Transport published its conclusions based on tests of 16 vehicles. It was revealed that one turned over during their investigations – but it wasn't a Suzuki. Their statement said: 'None exhibited handling characteristics that could automatically be regarded as unsafe. Drivers should realize that multi-purpose vehicles cannot be expected to handle on-road as well as modern passenger cars.' They called for manufacturers of 4x4 vehicles to issue driving and other safety advice to owners – though such information already formed a prominent part of the SJ owner's handbook material.

So the 'roll-over' issue was closed. At its heart was the difficulty of arriving at any satisfactory standard for car handling. The Americans have far more regulations governing car construction and performance than most European countries but have yet to devise a meaningful test for road behaviour. Vehicles designed for different purposes handle in different ways. As John Norman pointed out: 'If all the kinds of vehicles on our roads – heavy goods vehicles, vans, minibuses, cars towing caravans – had to be put through the disputed Consumer Union test there would be some very dramatic results!'

The lesson was clear: drive sensibly and within the limits of your vehicle. In Britain, Suzuki distributed a new guide, the *4x4 On Road Driving Booklet*, to every SJ owner. In America, the Samurai has a notice prominently displayed saying: 'It won't spoil the fun knowing that the Samurai handles differently from an ordinary passenger car. Avoid sharp turns and abrupt manoeuvres.'

The Rhino Club, established in 1984, gave Suzuki GB another way of spreading this message, though they were, in a sense, preaching to the converted. The Club, which any Suzuki 4x4 owner can enter free, was created as a social activity that allowed Suzuki GB to keep in touch with its owners.

Rallies organized at first on a regional basis and now developed to include an annual international event, the Rhino Rally, provided the opportunity for newcomers to learn techniques from off-road driving experts and take part in enjoyable competitions.

Use of the rhino motif was another idea of the British importers, since followed by their counterparts in other countries. It came about by chance, as the cars sent by the factory for the 1982 Birmingham Motor Show had plastic spare wheel covers carrying a drawing of a rhinocerous. They had used other

The Suzuki 4x4s are ideal for the narrow and rough roads of sunshine holiday islands, where many British motorists gain their first experience of them through hire fleets. The well-used LJ, right, is from Barbados, the Santana SJ410, below, in Ibiza.

The US-market Suzuki Samurai is the SJ413, available in convertible or, as here, hardtop version. Suzuki introduced the model to America in 1986.

symbols before, but the rhino appealed to Norman and Catford. They had it re-drawn and adopted it as a sign of toughness and dependability for the 4x4 range. This, in turn, led to support for the National Federation of Zoos and African conservation projects to protect real Black Rhinos.

An incidental benefit of the Rhino Club is that it has enabled Suzuki GB to build up a picture of the typical SJ410 owner. Contrary to what kerbside research in Chelsea might suggest, most are male and married, the SJ is one of two family cars, and it was chosen in preference to other, more expensive, four-wheel drive vehicles. Typically about one-fifth of an SJ's motoring is off-road.

There are, of course, both passenger and commercial versions of the Santana SJ410 and SJ413. The commercials, with 'blind' (covered) sides and without rear seats, are about £1,000 cheaper than their 'car' equivalents and genuine business users can also make a further saving by reclaiming the VAT (but even then, they can share the fun of a Suzuki in their leisure time). Ironically, in America a 1989 re-classification of imported vehicles labelled two-door 4x4s like the Samurai as trucks and imposed a 25% import tariff on them, while the bigger four-door ones, like the Range Rover, were allowed as multi-purpose vehicles carrying only a 2.5% tax.

In use, as opposed to arbitrary classification, it is clear that the small 4x4 market has moved towards the private buyer. More and more motorists value the idea of having a go-anywhere vehicle to negotiate country tracks or simply to be able to get around if the snow falls; the SJ forms a practical but entertaining alternative to a conventional second car. Realizing that, at the end of 1988, Suzuki launched the Vitara, a different kind of 4x4, more 'civilized' than the SJ and with a body style and interior closer to a conventional small car. They called it 'a car for new lifestyles' and *What Car?* magazine voted it Best All-Terrain Car for 1989. Except in being a small 4x4 with more or less the same transmission system, the Vitara owes little to the SJ series design. The engine is a new all-alloy 1.6-litre four-cylinder, the suspension is by coil springs and power steering is optional. While it may not have the ultimate off-road ability of the SJ, the Vitara can cope with pretty well any off-road

Putting on the style – 'Style' graphics were the metal-top SJ410VX counterpart to the Santana Sport soft-top introduced in 1988. The rhino motif appeared first on a spare wheel cover from Japan, but has since been adopted as a symbol by the British importers. Other animals have also featured; even a camel, as on the caravan opposite.

conditions that the average buyer is likely to encounter. For Suzuki it was important that even if this new 4x4 was more comfortable to ride in, and more car-like in its furnishings, it should still have the versatility of a fully fledged off-roader. 'These days, people have more diversified activities,' says managing director Yoshio Saito. 'While they may not actually do the outdoor things of

High-rise SJ. This caravan conversion, with all mod-cons, came from Switzerland for the 1987 Rhino Club Rally.

Low-rise version, below, is photographed to belie its size; it is a kiddy-sized SJ powered by an electric motor.

which the vehicle is capable, many buyers *wish* to do them.'

Suzuki now makes more than 1 million vehicles a year, 20% of which are 4x4s. Apart from the vehicles familiar to us, the Japanese SJ range includes a high-roof Jimny 1300 Panoramic Roof Wagon and a 550 EPi Turbo, still classified in the micro-car class but now with a four-stroke, three-cylinder 550cc engine with electronic fuel injection and turbocharger and developing 42bhp.

Some clues to the future direction of Suzuki's 4x4s can be seen from the experimental RT-1 displayed at the 1987 Tokyo Motor Show. This was a new interpretation of the 'sports off-roader', a mid-engined two-seater with four-wheel drive and high ground clearance, wide, but with skimpy buggy-type bodywork. In their Japanese way, Suzuki described the RT-1 as having 'live sports dynamics', part of a range of small, affordable cars that represent 'personal best'.

A new dimension – the Suzuki Vitara is intended to complement rather than displace the SJ-series. It combines off-road capability with saloon car comforts and sells in the price bracket above the SJ. Vitara is the European name; in Japan, it is called the Escudo, while in America the same vehicle is sold as the Suzuki Sidekick and, by General Motors, as the Geo Tracker.

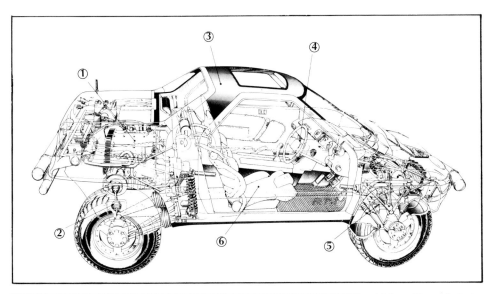

Vision of Suzuki's 4x4 future? The RT-1 concept car's main features: 1. 1.6-litre, 16-valve, fuel-injected engine with full-time four-wheel drive and six-speed gearbox. 2. Double trailing arm independent rear suspension. 3. Roof made of carbon-fibre, replacing roll-cage. 4. Computer guidance system. 5. Double-wishbone front suspension with horizontal dampers. 6. Specially moulded seats for enhanced comfort and water resistance.

Concept cars rarely find their way into production as shown, but after the Vitara, which meets the needs of those who want the SJ's versatility without its jeep style, a more obviously sporting 4x4 would seem a good way to go. We shall see. What is clear is that the market for four-wheel drive vehicles is expanding and that the 'sports/utility' 4x4s are the fastest growing sector (in Europe they grew 19% a year between 1979 and 1987). Among them, Suzuki have retained their position as suppliers of the best value-for-money, most economical, multi-purpose fun cars in the business.

Talking technical

Simple, strong and effective – that's the conclusion of Bob Cooke's technical examination of the Suzuki LJ and SJ variants

BOB COOKE is technical editor of *What Car?* but devotes much of his spare time to off-road activities. His early car testing was done on dirt roads in Rhodesia, where he was born. Even today, the tougher the conditions, the more he like them. He started writing about 4x4s for *Autocar* in the late 1970s.

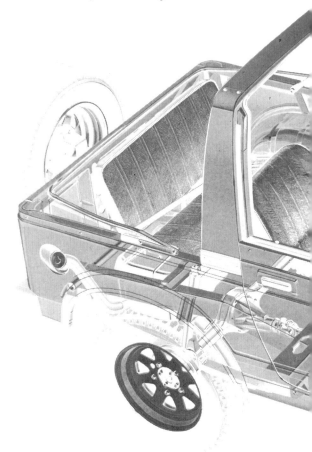

Suzuki's mini-jeep is in some ways a primitive machine. The early LJ80 looked it too, with its flat-panel body and corrugated door and tailgate panels standing high on ungainly-looking 16-inch wheels. The SJs, with their slightly longer wheelbase, wider track and more stylish bodies, look a lot more refined, but under that rakish grille, pretty paint job and attractive spoked wheels (now of better-proportioned 15in diameter) hides an old-fashioned mechanical layout. In the rough-and-tumble world of cross-country driving, though, being primitive is not necessarily a bad thing. Suzuki engineers obviously took a long, hard look at the Land Rovers of the time when putting together their own mighty-mouse mini-workhorse, for the little Suzuki has much in common with the world-beating British product.

Most importantly, the Suzuki uses a strong, rigid separate chassis of box-section steel, to which all the drive-train and suspension components are mounted. Such a chassis has the strength to resist bending and twisting forces as the car lurches through ruts and ditches, giving it a true rugged cross-country ability in back-breaking terrain where lesser machines such as the

Cutaway drawing of the SJ410 shows the elements that make this Suzuki a tough and versatile 4x4: box-section steel chassis carrying simple leaf-sprung beam axles and 970cc overhead-cam engine driving all four wheels via a central transfer box.

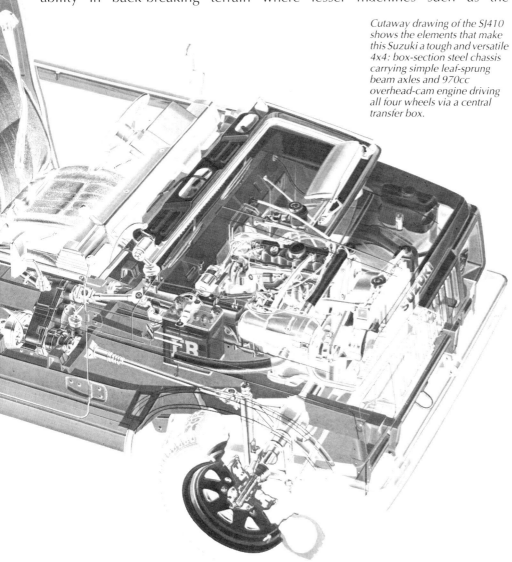

monocoque-design Lada Niva or Subaru 4x4 estates would suffer from twisting floorpans or buckled suspension mountings. The strong separate chassis also allows the use of a relatively lightweight body; it becomes feasible to use an open-topped body without having to resort to adding cumbersome stiffening reinforcement panels. So, right from the start, the SJ range included a choice of open runabout with canvas tilt and enclosed estate car or panel van.

When it comes to the Suzuki's suspension it is as well to remember that this diminutive 4x4 was conceived as a small working commercial vehicle, pure and simple. No-one was more surprised than Suzuki's own engineering and marketing men when their mechanical mules proved to be in great demand as steeds for today's rhinestone cowboys. For a commercial, hard-working vehicle, simple leaf springs all round, suspending the car on tough, rigid beam axles, are quite adequate. For all this apparent crudity, the Suzuki is in excellent company. At the time when the Suzuki off-roaders were on the drawing-board the all-conquering Land Rovers and market-leading Toyota Land Cruisers used semi-elliptic leaf springs all round, with strong beam axles front and rear, and several other relative newcomers, such as the Daihatsu Fourtrak and Nissan Patrol, followed suit in applying the same basic means of springing.

There are certainly some advantages in using leaf springs, but refinement in the quality of ride and consequent passenger comfort are not among them. Leaf springs are cheap and strong; they serve to locate the axles as well as to suspend them, therefore doing away with the necessity for other suspension components, such as the long leading and trailing arms required by off-road cars suspended on coil springs. The result is a system that is cheap to manufacture and strong enough to handle heavy-duty service – ideal qualities for commercial users.

The limitations of leaf springs in other areas are well known. Their heavy-duty nature combines with aspects like friction between the individual spring blades to make them unresponsive as the car runs over smallish bumps and ruts, so that the ride quality over such surfaces is decidedly harsh. When a lightly laden car, say with just driver and a passenger on board, hits a larger irregularity, the springs give much more readily, but also rebound strongly so that the car tends to bounce uncomfortably.

There are other, more fundamental issues. Since leaf springs run parallel to the front wheels, the amount of steering angle available to those wheels may be limited. The Suzuki has a 32ft turning circle, not wonderful for a car of 80-inch wheelbase – a Mini has the same wheelbase and gets round in 28ft.

The sophistication of all-coil suspension has reached few true working off-road vehicles; the Land Rover only recently followed the lead set by the Range Rover at its inception 16 years ago. But then, in a car of the Range Rover's class

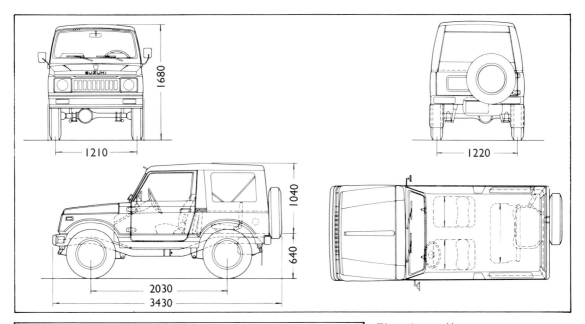

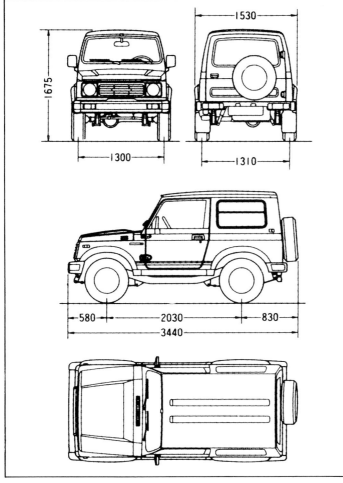

Dimensions and layout of the two SJ passenger vehicle variants – soft-top SJ410, above, and metal-top SJ413V JX. Measurements are in millimetres. 'Blind top' commercial versions, the SJ410QB and SJ413QB JA soft-tops and SJ410VB and SJ413VB JA hardtops, have the same dimensions.

SJ410 variations. On the left, Japanese-built SJ410V van and original SJ410Q soft-top. On the right, Spanish-built Santana SJ410VX metal-top and Santana SJ410QB soft-top.

– more a luxury estate than a farmyard workhorse – coil springs make more sense in spite of the extra cost involved in the additional suspension components since the improvement in ride comfort and refinement allowed by the more readily compliant coils is immediately obvious. The Land Rover, and notably the latest version of the Toyota Land Cruiser, use coils-all-round suspension only partly to ensure a more comfortable ride for passengers. Coils can allow an axle more vertical morement than more rigid semi-elliptics, and that is a boon – albeit a rather expensive one – in a true cross-country car. Coil springs do feature all round on one Suzuki all-terrain vehicle – their new 'recreational' car, the Vitara. The greater suspension refinement of this newcomer is, however, reflected quite clearly in its higher price compared with the more basic SJ.

Many other cross-country vehicles seeking a bite of the Range Rover and Land Rover market adopt a half-way approach, retaining the rugged simplicity of leaf springs on the rear axle, which, after all, takes most of the strain of heavy loads, while the front end is endowed with torsion-bar-sprung independence.

SJ413V JX metal-top, shown here in left-hand drive form, is made in Japan. Samurai name, carried on front wings, is used for model identification of this 1.3-litre version in some countries but not Britain.

Cars following this line include the Mitsubishi Shogun and Isuzu Trooper, but again these are far more expensive machines than the little Suzuki.

There is nothing primitive about the SJ's braking system, since all the SJ models get dual-circuit hydraulics, split front-rear, with disc front brakes. Drum brakes are used at the rear, but these are of the self-adjusting type. The Santana and 413 models also have servo assistance.

All the Suzuki off-roaders have the same type of steering, a recirculating-ball mechanism, damped to prevent the shock of running into ruts and bumps passing through to the driver's hands. Power assistance is a luxury that can't even be had as an extra, but the car is light enough and the steering low enough geared – over four turns from lock-to-lock in the 413 – not to need assistance.

The engines fitted to Suzuki SJ models available in Britain are all relatively low on power and performance, but are nonetheless well suited to the car's off-roading character.

For good off-road work, an all-terrain car needs an engine that gives strong pulling torque at low crankshaft speeds, to allow it to ease its way gently through slippery situations without allowing wheelspin to develop. The Land Rover 2.5-litre petrol engine, for instance, delivers its peak torque of 133lb/ft at a mere 2,000rpm. The Suzuki engines are all of long-stroke design, which favours good torque, but sheer lack of cubic capacity robs them of true muscle.

The LJ80 was powered by a 797cc overhead-camshaft engine developing a mere 39bhp, with 44lb/ft torque available at 3,500rpm. No wonder the SJs

All LJ and SJ models use
simple leaf springs for
front and rear
suspension. SJ413,
shown here, uses
multi-leaf springs,
whereas Santana has
basically a single leaf
arrangement. Note, too,
from this illustration of
the rear suspension, that
later SJ413s have the
handbrake operating on
the rear drum brakes
rather than on the
prop-shaft as in the
SJ410.

Generous ground
clearance, a short
wheelbase and minimal
body overhangs mean
that the SJ is able to ride
bumps and clear
obstacles that defeat less
rugged machines. This
diagram shows its
maximum approach and
departure angles.

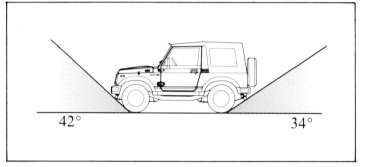

brought into Britain feature larger engines; it ought to be remembered, though, that a 534cc, 27bhp version is available in other markets.

The SJ410 has a 970cc unit capable of delivering 45bhp, and 54lb/ft of torque at 3,000rpm. Obviously punchier is the 1,324cc engine in the SJ413, with 64bhp on tap, but although peak torque of 74lb/ft sounds quite good in such a lightweight vehicle, it is delivered at a rather high 3,500rpm.

These engines are all of conventional design – four-cylinder in-line and water-cooled, with belt-driven single overhead cam operating two valves per cylinder. In the case of the smaller engines, the block is of cast iron with an aluminium alloy head, but the 1,324cc unit is a newer, higher-revving, smoother-running, all-alloy design – it is in fact a slightly detuned version of the engine that powers the Suzuki Swift supermini. Other off-road cars that take power from thinly disguised roadgoing car engines suffer to some extent from the same problem of not having enough low-down slogging torque – most notable being the prestigious Mercedes-Benz G-wagen, which serves far better as a highway cruiser than a slippery-terrain off-roader.

The lack of outright performance from any of the Suzuki engines could be seen by some as something of an inconvenience, since the SJ410's maximum speed of 66mph means it can't be cruised at the legal speed limit on motorways; even the SJ413 can only break that limit by just 5mph. In fact, the power has been purposely limited to ensure that the cars cannot be driven at speeds above which, by their very nature, they might become unstable. The narrow track, short wheelbase, long-travel suspension and high stance don't add up to a recipe for cruising stability.

The Japanese-built SJ410 models drive through four-speed transmissions. Once again the choice of gearing reflects the vehicles' purely functional nature; the ratios are low, as befits a vehicle that might have to haul heavy loads over rough terrain. More fashion-conscious, on-road users have found the lack of a fifth gear to be a disadvantage because the car becomes quite noisy when driving at speed. Fortunately, the bigger-engined SJ413 gets a five-speed gearbox, with the top gear serving as a mild overdrive, allowing much more peaceful cruising.

Good news, too, for those who are happy with the less powerful and more economical SJ410. An agreement between Suzuki Motor Company and Land Rover's Santana factory near Linares, in Spain, sees Suzuki SJ410 models being assembled alongside Land Rovers in that country. This allows Suzuki GB Ltd to import Spanish-built SJ410s without contravening the restrictions on Japanese car imports and thus increase the total number of cars they have to sell. Though these Spanish models are essentially identical to the Japanese-built SJ410s, Suzuki took the opportunity to make a few alterations to suit recreational rather than commercial users. Thus the Santana-origin models have softer spring rates in an effort to improve on-road ride comfort, and they also have five-speed transmissions. These Spanish-built models proudly bear the Santana badge and cost a few hundred pounds more than the Japanese-origin SJ410, usually featuring special paintwork and interior trim to make them more appealing to recreational owners.

All SJs have a substantial damper built into the steering system to insulate the driver from the shocks of off-road driving. Power steering is not available, but the effort required at the wheel is not a problem, on or off-road.

All the Suzukis have the same four-wheel drive system. It follows the general pattern adopted by most all-terrain cars in that drive is normally to the rear wheels alone, but can be added to the front wheels at any time by engaging the dog clutch in the transfer case.

In the Suzuki, the engine and its associated gearbox are mounted quite high over the chassis. Though this does raise the centre of gravity to some extent, it means that the complicated and expensive mechanical heart of the vehicle is kept well out of the way of possible damage from jutting rocks, and is less likely to be flooded when fording streams.

The output from the main gearbox enters the top of the transfer gearbox, which has a choice of high- or low-ratio gearing, and is taken down to a level which is closer to the car's axle line, but still high enough to be protected to some extent by the chassis-frame side members. From this lower level, drive shafts run to front and rear axles. These are offset slightly to the right in both cases, a point which ought to be borne in mind when easing over a rocky outcrop; keeping the rock to the left of the car's centre-line will reduce the chance of cracking the front differential, which is, effectively, the most vulnerable mechanical component.

Such a selectable four-wheel drive system has the advantage of simplicity and cheapness. More advanced off-road cars such as the modern Land Rovers have adopted permanent four-wheel drive, an ideal arrangement with two main advantages – firstly, the driver is relieved of any requirement to make a decision about whether or not four-wheel drive should be engaged, and secondly, four-wheel drive is always there when it is needed. Such a system requires the added expense of a third differential gearset, though, to allow for rotational differences between front and rear wheels. There are also disadvantages, though, the main one being that since the forward propeller shaft and axle shafts are constantly being driven, even when cruising on firm-surfaced roads, the extra frictional and inertial forces exerted by these components saps a percentage – albeit a small one – of the engine's power and, hence, increases fuel consumption. There is also an argument that front tyres wear a little more quickly because they are constantly handling driving forces as well as steering inputs.

The Suzuki's selectable system manages without the expense of the central differential, but that does mean that four-wheel drive should be engaged only when the surface becomes slippery. Since there is no means of eliminating those rotational differences between front and rear wheels, driving in 4x4 mode on a firm surface will result in strain building up in the transmission – an effect known as transmission wind-up – which could become serious enough to damage the transfer box. Some of the transmission strain might find its way out of the system by forcing tyres to skid, which in turn will lead to far worse tyre wear than would happen in any permanent four-wheel drive arrangement.

Also, since rotational differences between front and rear wheels occur mainly when steering through a curve, the system tends to lock solid when attempting to make a turn on a firm surface – such as when trying to park – if four-wheel drive is engaged.

Nor does the mere fact of having selectable four-wheel drive eliminate the problem of excess fuel use because of the movement of the front-running drive shafts. Even when four-wheel drive is disengaged in the Suzuki, the front axle shafts and forward prop-shaft rotate, back-driven by the whirling front wheels, adding drag as well as frictional and inertial wastage. The answer lies in a useful optional extra, well worth the £88 or so – a set of freewheeling front hubs. Simply turning a small thumbscrew in each hub disconnects it from the drive shaft, allowing the shafts to come to rest when proceeding in two-wheel drive mode. The only snag is that before four-wheel drive can be reselected the hubs have to be re-engaged. Failure to do so will mean that even though the transfer case lever is in the four-wheel drive position, the front-drive components will merely spin uselessly, leaving the car effectively and deceptively still in two-wheel drive.

Care should be taken, too, not to attempt to engage four-wheel drive while on the move if freewheel hubs are disengaged, since this would involve linking the spinning rear drive shaft with a stationary forward one – ouch! Once the hubs are engaged, however, or in a car lacking the freewheel facility, it is quite possible to shift between two and four-wheel drive while on the move.

Heart of the first Suzuki 4x4 to appear in Britain – the LJ80's 797cc overhead-cam four-cylinder was a modern design that led directly to the larger-capacity engines of the SJ series.

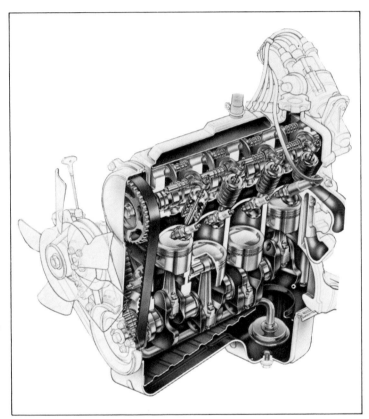

SJ413's 64bhp G13A 1.3-litre engine has an aluminium-alloy cylinder block and head and is related to that which powers the Suzuki Swift hatchback. SJ410's 45bhp 970cc unit, shown underbonnet, has a cast-iron block.

Looking closely at the SJ range's mechanical layout, one might justifiably be surprised at the car's patent popularity among non-commercial users. The point is, however, that for all its lack of refinement, the SJ is a very effective all-terrain car. It has ruggedly attractive good looks and it oozes character, which for many fashion-conscious drivers are attributes that far outweigh limitations in performance and ride comfort. And furthermore, those who actually take their Suzukis off the road find the cars well up to the task of providing thrilling rough-and-tumble action, and strong enough to shrug off heavy-handed cross-country driving with impunity.

Specifications

MODEL	LJ80
ENGINE	4-cylinder
	797cc
	Alloy head
	Iron block
	Water-cooled
	Fixed fan
Bore/stroke	60 x 66mm
Compression ratio	8.7:1
Valve gear	OHC, belt drive
Max power	40bhp at 5,500 rpm
Max torque	44lb/ft at 3,500rpm
Fuel type	2-star, unleaded
Carburettor	Single-choke
	Mikuni-Solex
Battery	35AH
Alternator	35A

TRANSMISSION		
Type	4-speed manual,	
	all-synchromesh,	
	2-speed transfer	
Main ratios	Top	1.0
	3rd	1.54
	2nd	2.36
	1st	3.84
	Reverse	4.03
Transfer ratios	High	1.56
	Low	2.58
Final drive	4.55	

SUSPENSION	
Front	
– Springs	Live axle / Semi-elliptic
– Dampers	Telescopic
– Anti-roll bar	No
Rear	
– Springs	Live axle / Semi-elliptic
– Dampers	Telescopic
– Anti-roll bar	No

STEERING	
Type	Recirculating-ball
Wheel diameter	16in
Turns lock-to-lock	2.9

BRAKES	Hydraulic, dual circuit, split front/rear
Front	Drum
Rear	Drum
Servo	No
Parking brake	Drum on prop-shaft

WHEELS	
Type	Pressed-steel
Rim width	4.5in
Tyres	Tubed crossply, 6.00 x 16

EQUIPMENT	
Windscreen wipers	2-speed
Interior heater	Water valve
Radio	No
Digital clock	No
Head restraints	No
Seat upholstery	PVC
Floor covering	PVC mats
Body protection moulding	No
Spare wheel cover	No
Spare wheel lock	No
Passenger door mirror	Yes
Lamp guards	No
Underbody protection	Galvanized steel, vinyl sealant

MODEL	SJ410
ENGINE	4-cylinder
	970cc
	Alloy head
	Iron block
	Water-cooled
	Fixed fan
Bore/stroke	65.5 x 72mm
Compression ratio	8.8:1
Valve gear	OHC, belt drive
Max power	45bhp at 5,500 rpm
Max torque	54lb/ft at 3,000rpm
Fuel type	2-star, unleaded
Carburettor	Single-choke
	Mikuni-Solex
Battery	35AH
Alternator	35A

TRANSMISSION

Type	4-speed manual,
	all-synchromesh
	2-speed transfer
Main ratios	Top 1.0
	3rd 1.42
	2nd 1.95
	1st 3.14
	Reverse 3.47
Transfer ratios	High 1.58
	Low 2.51
Final drive	4.11

SUSPENSION

Front	Live axle
– Springs	Semi-elliptic
– Dampers	Telescopic
– Anti-roll bar	No
Rear	Live axle
– Springs	Semi-elliptic
– Dampers	Telescopic
– Anti-roll bar	No

STEERING

Type	Recirculating-ball
Wheel diameter	15.5in
Turns lock-to-lock	3.4

BRAKES

	Hydraulic, dual
	circuit, split
	front/rear
Front	Disc
Rear	Drum
Servo	No
Parking brake	Drum on prop-shaft

WHEELS

Type	Spoked steel
Rim width	5.5in
Tyres	Radial
	195SR-15

EQUIPMENT

Windscreen wipers	2-speed + intermittent
Interior heater	Water valve
Radio	AM mono
Digital clock	No
Head restraints	No
Seat upholstery	Fabric
Floor covering	Carpet
Body protection	
moulding	Yes
Spare wheel cover	No
Spare wheel lock	No
Passenger door mirror	Yes
Lamp guards	No
Underbody protection	Galvanized steel,
	vinyl sealant

MODEL	SJ410 Santana
ENGINE	4-cylinder
	970cc
	Alloy head
	Iron block
	Water-cooled
	Fixed fan
Bore/stroke	65.5 x 72mm
Compression ratio	8.8:1
Valve gear	OHC, belt drive
Max power	45bhp at 5,500 rpm
Max torque	54lb/ft at 3,000rpm
Fuel type	2-star, unleaded
Carburettor	Single-choke
	Mikuni-Solex
Battery	35AH
Alternator	35A

TRANSMISSION

Type	5-speed manual,
	all-synchromesh
	2-speed transfer
Main ratios	Top 0.79
	4th 1.0
	3rd 1.42
	2nd 1.95
	1st 3.16
	Reverse 3.47
Transfer ratios	High 1.58
	Low 2.51
Final drive	4.11

SUSPENSION

Front	Live axle
– Springs	Semi-elliptic
– Dampers	Telescopic
– Anti-roll bar	No
Rear	Live axle
– Springs	Semi-elliptic
– Dampers	Telescopic
– Anti-roll bar	No

STEERING

Type	Recirculating-ball
Wheel diameter	15.5in
Turns lock-to-lock	3.4

BRAKES

	Hydraulic, dual circuit, split front/rear
Front	Disc
Rear	Drum
Servo	Yes
Parking brake	Drum on prop-shaft

WHEELS

Type	Spoked steel
Rim width	5.5in
Tyres	Radial 195SR-15

EQUIPMENT

Windscreen wipers	2-speed + flick wipe
Interior heater	Water valve
Radio	No
Digital clock	No
Head restraints	Yes
Seat upholstery	Fabric
Floor covering	Carpet
Body protection moulding	No
Spare wheel cover	Yes
Spare wheel lock	Yes
Passenger door mirror	Yes
Lamp guards	Yes
Underbody protection	Galvanized steel, vinyl sealant

MODEL

SJ413

ENGINE

	4-cylinder 1,324cc Alloy head Alloy block Water-cooled Viscous fan
Bore/stroke	74 x 77mm
Compression ratio	8.9:1
Valve gear	OHC, belt drive
Max power	63bhp at 6,000 rpm
Max torque	73lb/ft at 3,500rpm
Fuel type	2-star, unleaded
Carburettor	Double-choke Mikuni-Solex
Battery	35AH
Alternator	35A

TRANSMISSION

Type	5-speed manual, all-synchromesh 2-speed transfer
Main ratios	Top 0.79
	4th 1.0
	3rd 1.42
	2nd 1.95
	1st 3.65
	Reverse 3.47
Transfer ratios	High 1.41
	Low 2.27
Final drive	3.91

SUSPENSION

Front	Live axle
– Springs	Semi-elliptic
– Dampers	Telescopic
– Anti-roll bar	Yes
Rear	Live axle
– Springs	Semi-elliptic
– Dampers	Telescopic
– Anti-roll bar	No

STEERING

Type	Recirculating-ball
Wheel diameter	15.5in
Turns lock-to-lock	4.2

BRAKES

	Hydraulic, dual circuit, split front/rear
Front	Disc
Rear	Drum
Servo	Yes
Parking brake	On rear drums

WHEELS

Type	Spoked steel
Rim width	5.5in
Tyres	Radial 205/70-15

EQUIPMENT

Windscreen wipers	2-speed + intermittent
Interior heater	Water valve
Radio	AM mono
Digital clock	Yes
Head restraints	Yes
Seat upholstery	Fabric
Floor covering	Carpet
Body protection moulding	Yes
Spare wheel cover	No
Spare wheel lock	No
Passenger door mirror	No
Lamp guards	No
Underbody protection	Galvanized steel, vinyl sealant

Euro-SJ assessed

The SJ410, built in Spain, is Suzuki's lowest-priced 4x4. Bob Cooke gives an SJ410 Santana Sport a thorough work-out, on and off-road

Britain is hardly a country where one would imagine that off-road driving would feature largely as a recreational occupation. Yet the Suzuki SJs quickly entered the cross-country best-seller league, appealing just as much to the fashion-conscious city dweller as to farmers seeking a lightweight, cheaper and more economical second car to their trusty old Land Rover.

What the 'recreational' buyers saw in the car was its rugged, muscular looks, echoing – albeit in miniature – the character of the luxurious and elegant Range Rover. Yet in some ways it could hardly be less suited to the role of city runabout – not much power from the small engine and a harsh ride from the basic suspension. For all that, demand remains high, and an increasing number of 'city off-roaders' are discovering at first hand the thrills and enjoyment of real cross-country adventuring.

With demand increasing but the supply of new models from Japan limited by a 'gentlemen's agreement' restricting imports, Suzuki sought – and found – a loophole. An agreement with the Land Rover Santana factory at Linares in Spain bought the right to have Suzuki SJ410s built alongside Land Rovers there, and cars of European origin could of course be imported into Britain without restriction.

The opportunity was taken, however, to try and tune the Spanish-built SJ models better to suit the requirements of the British recreational market.

The interior was given a less utilitarian look by fitting more substantial seats with better padding, featuring built-in head restraints. There are matching cloth inserts in the door trim panels and carpeting stretching all the way through to the load bay. Where Japanese-built roadgoing 410 models had a rather basic bench seat in the rear, the Santana is fitted with a more comfortable pair of seats which can be folded up individually or together to increase luggage capacity in the rear.

The suspension remains cart-spring all round, but in an effort to improve the quality of ride, the spring rates have been softened, and to improve the car's highway cruising, a five-speed gearbox is fitted with an overdrive top ratio. The engine, however, is the same 970cc unit fitted to the Japanese-built 410.

The Santana was originally offered only in open soft-top form. There were two versions, the Santana and the Santana Sport; there was no actual

Rear seat passengers get an open-air ride in the Santana Sport. The driver and front seat passenger, shielded by side windows and central pillars, can stay cosy with the top down even in cool weather.

mechanical or equipment difference between these, the only distinguishing feature being the paintwork. The Santana was white with grey and yellow side striping, and the Sport black with red-striped grey side panels. Later, only Sport versions were offered, but in a choice of Crystal Silver with black soft-top or red with a white soft-top. More recently, hardtop estate versions of the Santana have joined the range.

The dashboard on the Santana differs in detail from that of the SJ410. The basic moulding stretching across the bulkhead is the same, with two ventilation outlets in the middle and one more at each end, a grab handle on the passenger side protruding from above the locking glove box and a small central console housing the heating and ventilation controls and the slot for a radio. Usually, SJ410 and 413 models were sold with a radio as part of the standard equipment, a Japanese-fitment AM-only push-button mono set. The Spanish-built Santana lacks this feature, leaving the choice of in-car entertainment to the purchaser, but the Santana does at least have an aerial mounted on the front screen pillar. A range of Clarion stereo cassette units is available as a dealer option.

The instrument panel on the Santana differs slightly from that on the Japanese 410. The dials are housed in a rectangular panel bolted on to the dashboard, speedometer to the left and a matching circular housing on the right containing fuel, water temperature and battery condition gauges with a

Instrument panel of the Santana, above, shows a number of improvements from the original Japanese-built SJ410, left. Note that, in addition to the repositioning of the controls and instruments, the Spanish product offers five gears instead of four.

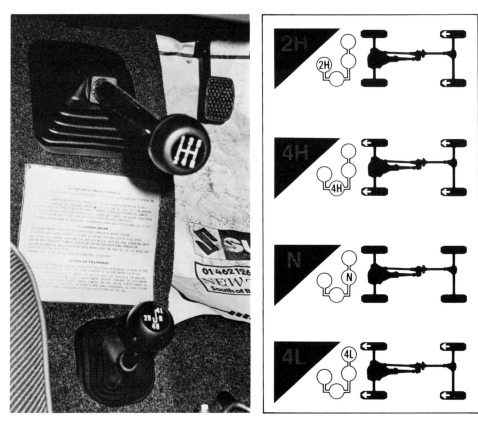

The key to the Suzuki's four-wheel drive system. The transfer lever, located just behind the gear lever, offers four positions, the functions of which are illustrated to the right. Santana instruction panel starts off with Spanish wording, but provides translations in English and French.

selection of warning lamps scattered between them.

Small as the Suzuki is, it is still quite a step up into the cabin. It stands high, with 8in of ground clearance, and there's still a couple of inches of sill to step over. For all the Santana's extra cloth and carpeting, there is still a purely functional look to the interior – for instance, in the way the seat mountings with their fore-aft sliding mechanism stand prominently out in the open. The seats themselves, though boasting better padding than those fitted in the Japanese 410, are still rather simple in construction; though comfortable enough, they are a little on the small side and lack support for the thighs and laterally – not a problem in short drives around town, but noticeable when lurching about in the rough.

The controls are simple and straightforward, with pedals that look far too small for a real off-road vehicle hanging down behind the dashboard, and a long, chunky gear lever protruding from the transmission tunnel. The steering wheel is a sensible 15.5in diameter, though of an odd typically Japanese-looking three-spoke design. There is, of course, a second gear lever set in the floor behind the main lever. This is the transfer selector, and works in exactly the same way as in other Suzuki off-roaders. It sits normally in the 2H position – that's two-wheel drive, high ratio, the setting that should be chosen whenever the car is driven on the road or on firm, reasonably level off-road areas.

When the surface becomes slippery – ice or slush on the road or mud or wet grass off the road – shifting the lever rearwards and a little to the left selects four-wheel drive, but still high ratio. When steep inclines have to be tackled, low ratio can be selected by easing the transfer lever further to the left and forwards; it passes through a neutral position on the way so it's essential to ensure that the low-ratio gear has been engaged before attempting to drive away. Low ratio cannot be engaged without first selecting four-wheel drive.

Access to the rear seats is easy enough if the soft-top is off and passengers are agile enough to clamber straight over the side, using the back tyres as steps. More normally, though, rear seat passengers have to squeeze through behind

A more comfortable place to be. The Santana specification includes more elaborate trim than in the original SJ410 with well upholstered and nicely trimmed seats, matching door panels and full carpeting.

*Santana Sport has
separate rear seats with
reasonable legroom,
though luggage space
behind is minimal.
Earlier SJ410s had a
bench seat, as shown in
the 1983 metal top
version, right.*

the front seats, an awkward manoeuvre because the door opening is quite
small and the door angles forwards along the lower half of its trailing edge. As
on many Japanese designs, people are encouraged to enter through the
passenger door – the one that would normally be facing the pavement if the car
is parked normally – by an arrangement that allows the front seat on that side
to slide forwards easily and quickly as the backrest is tipped down, thus
revealing a more passable gap.

The rear seats are reasonably well padded in the Santana; their only problem
is that, like the front ones, they are physically small. Legroom is not too bad,

though; the rear seats have deliberately been mounted quite far back to ensure reasonable passenger comfort even though this cuts luggage space behind the seats to a minimum. If the car is to be used as a load-carrier the rear seats fold up. They won't stay there of their own accord, though – unless the cargo is substantial enough to hold them in place – so little straps are provided on the door pillar which stretch over and fasten to a stud on the seat base.

The fabric roof is simple enough to remove and replace, its best feature in this area being its relatively small size and light weight. A single supporting strut angles back from just behind the central pillar, which doubles as a roll-over protection bar. This strut has a short knuckle joint at its base which locks in place to tension the fabric tilt cover. Removing the roof begins with releasing this joint to relax tension on the fabric, after which the studs along the sides and

1987 'all white' Santana shows how rear seats fold individually to increase the load space while the front passenger seat has a 'walk-in' forward tip to facilitate access to the back.

Buffers on the windscreen rail sit on the bonnet when the screen is hinged forward for real wind-in-the-hair motoring, vintage sports car style. Sticker shows that the car provided for photography, as some others in this book, was kindly provided by Suzuki dealer New Tudor, of Bromley, Kent.

around the back are popped apart. Velcro tabs hold the cloth to the tensioning strut and the roll-over bar, and after releasing these the cloth may be pulled away from the securing rail across the top of the front screen. The supporting strut folds down, but not completely out of the way, so rear seat passengers should take care to avoid it when being driven over rough terrain as it can bounce around and could catch an unwary finger or knuckle.

On the open road, speed is not this car's strong point. The fault lies not entirely in the small engine with its relatively low power output, but with the bluff-fronted, box-like styling which has the car running into a sort of aerodynamic brick wall at around 60mph. In the overdrive fifth gear the Santana Sport is hard pressed to hold 62mph; anything remotely resembling an upward incline will see the speedo needle winding its way quickly back around the dial. In fourth, which is a more usable top ratio, the Santana will howl up to 68mph, but even then it needs a level stretch to maintain that speed – and the accompanying noise from the straining power plant soon becomes quite tiring.

On a downhill stretch, speed can build up in quite exhilarating fashion, but don't be fooled by the speedometer, which can be at least 10mph optimistic when reading 80mph – at which point the car has just touched 70mph true.

Under the circumstances, the Santana Sport is hardly at home on the motorway, where it is too slow to join the scurry in the overtaking lane. It is, however, just a little bit faster than most occupants of the left-hand lane, resulting in many long-drawn-out overtaking manoeuvres that will test the

Camshaft cover carries Suzuki-Santana wording. Underbonnet accessibility is good and electrical components are kept high up to protect them from water thrown up from underneath. The owner is provided with a manual and a small tool-kit. The lockable glove box is appreciated in an open vehicle.

patience both of the Suzuki driver and that of the drivers caught up behind.

Acceleration feels better than it is, since the little Suzuki lurches and bounces about excitedly when driven quickly away from the traffic lights. In fact, the Santana Sport takes a very leisurely 30.2 seconds to get to 60mph, performance which demands that the car be driven hard all the time just to keep up with the general run of busy city traffic.

In performance terms, the Suzuki feels more capable away from the motorway on quieter, slower country roads, but these highlight its rather vague handling. Because the Santana is designed as an off-road car, the suspension is arranged to allow plenty of vertical – and some sideways – movement of the wheels. The recirculating-ball steering also lacks crispness; this again is designed into the car to prevent the effects of running into a sharp bump in cross-country driving from jerking the steering wheel out of the driver's hand, or perhaps wrenching a wrist. There's a hydraulic damper to take the shock out of those bumps – but it also takes much of the feel out of the steering. The overall result of this is that the car tends to wander about a bit when running straight, and its response can be somewhat unpredictable when steered through a bend at speed. Keeping the car in control on a winding country road calls for speed to be kept down and a firm grip on the steering wheel.

The Santana has softer springing than the Japanese-made 410, but the suspension is still firm enough to make for bumpy, bouncy and joggly progress over roads with less-than-perfect surfaces. A bump in the middle of a corner can have the car hopping sideways with a combination of bounce and body roll.

These aspects of the car's handling are no more than might be expected in a car with good off-road ability, and will be understood by owners planning to use the car as a recreational off-roader. It is important, though, that newcomers to off-road vehicles and owners intending to use the car purely as an on-road runabout should understand the limitations and not attempt to exceed the car's handling capabilities, nor should they expect too much in the way of ride comfort from a car in its original specification. It is possible to improve the quality of ride comfort, but this involves replacing the dampers – various alternatives are available, see Chapter 7.

So the Santana Sport is by no means a refined and comfortable highway cruiser, but it makes a great short-distance round-town runabout. It is an easy enough car to drive, with a surprisingly light clutch, and though the gearshift can be a bit notchy, it's light enough in action. The steering, too, for all its vagueness of feel, is not particularly heavy; it may take a bit of muscle to get the car in and out of a tight parking space, but once on the move the steering weight is quite manageable.

The Santana Sport also makes a great off-road fun-car. All those things that detract from the car's on-road agility and stability become positive factors when the car is driven as it was designed to be used – away from the tarmac, out in the carefree rough-and-tumble of cross-country driving.

Off-road driving is usually all about lots of low-speed, gutsy engine torque. The 970cc Suzuki engine doesn't have an awful lot of that – 54lb/ft at 3,000rpm compared with 133lb/ft at 2,000rpm in a four-cylinder Land Rover – but then the Suzuki's lower weight and smaller dimensions make up for the engine's lack of lugging ability.

Lots of gears usually helps, too, since the more chance a driver has of matching the car's ground speed with the engine's peak torque point the better the chance of fuss-free progress over a wide range of difficult conditions. A five-speed gearbox – giving a total of 10 available ratios when combined with the dual-range transfer box – sounds desirable, but in the Santana's case there's little advantage over the four-speed transmission in the Japanese 410 since in practice the only usable gear when conditions get rough is low-range second. First is just a little too low to cope with loose surfaces, since wheelspin develops too easily; third is too high for tackling slippery slopes, leaving the little engine too prone to stalling for lack of power.

Generally speaking, it is second gear to tackle an obstacle such as a steep incline or a stretch of cloying mud, then back into top when the surface levels off and firms up again. The overdrive fifth gear does at least allow the Santana to reach a slightly faster cross-country cruising speed in the low range, reducing the need to shift back up to into high range when running over smoother, firmer ground. Not that shifting between high and low is a problem, apart from the need to ensure that the transfer box is actually engaged; it is possible to accidentally leave the transfer lever in the neutral slot, which could be embarrassing – and even dangerous – if the intention was to engage low range to ensure controlled progress under engine braking down a long and slippery steep descent.

The short wheelbase also gives the Suzuki an advantage over some bigger off-roaders, since it allows the car to negotiate more tortuous terrain without grounding in front, at the rear, or on the floorpan; the Suzuki has just a little more actual ground clearance than a Land Rover, but the short wheelbase gives it effectively much more when topping a rise.

The Santana Sport – like all models in the Suzuki LJ and SJ range – definitely feels more at home off the road than on a metalled surface. Without doubt it is one of the best budget-priced off-road cars for a beginner or occasional mud-plugger to use as an enjoyable recreational cross-country vehicle; it has enough ability and more than enough strength to cope. But that doesn't mean a fashion-conscious owner looking purely for a modish city runabout will be making a bad choice. In either case, the Santana is reasonably priced and with insurance rates comparable with those for a Ford Escort Popular and fuel consumption of 31 mpg possible in general driving, it is economical enough for younger drivers.

Performance – SJ410 Santana					
Maximum speeds		**Acceleration from rest**		**Acceleration in 4th and 5th**	
5th	62mph	0–30mph	5.5 sec	mph	4th sec	5th sec
4th	66mph	0–40	9.9	20–40	13.2	19.3
3rd	55mph	0–50	10.1	30–50	15.5	24.5
2nd	40mph	0–60	30.4	40–60	24.0	43.4
1st	25mph					

Overall fuel consumption – 27.0mpg
Source: *Motor*, August 22 1987

More power, wider stance

Bob Cooke tests the SJ413, also known as the Samurai, which combines a more powerful 1.3-litre engine with a wider track

The word 'Samurai' over the front wing, where on other Suzuki SJs you find the indicator repeater flasher, is the first clue. Then you might notice the horizontal grille pattern instead of the usual vertical bars. A trained eye might also notice the slightly lower-profile tyres, 205/70-15 radials instead of the usual 195SR-15s; they add up to a Suzuki with a lot more muscle.

Anyone who took exception to the bouncy, hard ride of the Suzuki SJ410 would probably not have got as far as complaining about the lack of power. The diehards, though – the true enthusiasts, whether they used their cars on or off the road – would appreciate the reason for the Suzuki's unrefined ride quality, but may well have felt there was something lacking in a more important area – under the bonnet. Hence the appearance of a 1,324cc engine in the Suzuki SJ line-up, offering the possibility of a punchier alternative to the hard-worked 970cc mini-motor in the 410.

The bigger-capacity engine appears in the Suzuki 413; in later models the 413 badging is replaced by the more evocative Samurai name. Whatever the badging, in most respects the 413 is mechanically identical to the 410. There are minor differences; though the other ratios of the five-speed box are similar to those in the five-speed 410 Santana, there is a lower first which, linked with higher gearing in the transfer box and a higher final drive, gives longer gearing for faster, more relaxed cruising, but also leaves an acceptably low bottom gear that effectively broadens the span of gearing – useful for off-road driving.

There is the same strong, separate steel box-section chassis, cart springs all round and servo-assisted brakes, discs in front and self-adjusting drums at the rear. As on the 410 models, drive is normally to the rear wheels, but can be added to the fronts by engaging the transfer lever. Manually-operated freewheeling front hubs are again an option; if fitted, these would have to be

SJ413, opposite, is distinguished by horizontal grille slats and Samurai badges on the front wings. Under the bonnet, left, is a 1.3-litre engine with distinctive carburettor plenum chamber and a large air filter canister alongside.

SJ413V JX interior is more elaborately equipped than the Santana's with a centre facia console, distinctive steering wheel design and more supportive seats.

twisted into engagement before four-wheel drive can effectively be applied to the front wheels.

The 1.3-litre engine is of thoroughly conventional but modern design. It is an all-alloy four-cylinder unit with a single overhead camshaft operating two valves per cylinder. Fuelling is via a twin-choke downdraught carburettor and the compression ratio of 8.9:1 is low enough to allow the car to run on two-star petrol.

The engine is in fact a slightly detuned version of that used in the Suzuki Swift hatchback, and being designed primarily for road use it is not ideally suited to use in an off-road vehicle since the peak torque and power are developed too high in the rev range – the engine will produce 63bhp at 6,000rpm and 73lb/ft at 3,500rpm. This means a relative lack of flexibility, which in any serious workhorse off-road vehicle would be seen as a failing, but in a car like this little Suzuki with purely light-duty or recreational potential it is much more acceptable. Especially when the effective result is an improvement in the car's performance and behaviour, both on and off the road.

Obviously, a more powerful engine offering greater road speed, and improving the car's overall appeal as a fashionable on-road runabout, called for revisions to the suspension to reduce the harsh ride and lack of handling precision of the 410. Hence the 413 has softer spring rates and more compliant damping than 410 and Santana models and the front axle takes an anti-roll bar to improve the car's poise in cornering. Later models have also gained 2.75in in the track, mainly through having wider tyres fitted – 205/70-15 Dunlop radials instead of the original 195SR-15 Michelins – and have a stiffer anti-roll bar, both features aimed at improving on-road handling.

Detailed styling differences like that neat grille and Samurai badge apart, the

One-piece metal rear door is supported open by a gas strut and a right-hand hinge for safe loading at the kerb in countries that drive on the left.

obvious feature about the Suzuki SJ413 that sets it apart from the Santana Sport is that it is available only in hardtop form – obviously robbing the owner of the fun of open-air cross-country driving, but offering better isolation from noise and full protection from the elements. In a country like Britain, where opportunities for fun in the sun are limited indeed, this makes the solid roof a blessing in disguise. The 413 also has neatly colour-keyed wheelarch extensions linked by a protective rubbing strip running along the sills.

The 413 is seen as the top-of-the-range SJ model, and its price and interior equipment reflect that.

Inside, the early Samurai models featured a facia broadly similar to that used in the 410 and Santana; an upper section housing four round ventilation outlets and a bolt-on instrument panel, with a hang-on grip rail for the front seat passenger above the locking glovebox, and an ashtray and the heating and ventilation controls in the centre, just above the standard-sized slot for the radio. The steering wheel, too, was identical to that used in the 410. The main difference lay in the better instrumentation – a digital clock in the centre of the dash panel, and an instrument panel containing a rev-counter and separate fuel level and water temperature gauges.

The later Samurai has a whole new look with a much more stylish facia. The ventilation outlets are there, but bigger and rectangular; the passenger still gets a grab rail above the glove locker. The instrument panel still has the rev-counter and the separate gauges, but there's a chunky central console as well. The equipment housed there is the same – digital clock, heater controls and the radio – but it is all presented in a much better way.

There is cloth trim on the seats and door panels, and carpeting underfoot. The seats are more supportive than those in the 410 or Santana, featuring chunky side-wings to hold occupants more firmly when cornering or when lurching about in the rough. The seats have built-in head restraints of hollow-centred see-through design, and the backrests are fully reclining.

The controls are the same as on smaller-engined SJs, except for the snazzy four-spoke steering wheel on the latest Samurai versions, with the same two gear levers protruding from the floor; the transfer lever has the same 2H-4H-N-4L pattern. Switchgear conforms to the usual Japanese pattern with a right-hand steering column stalk working the headlamps, dipswitch and indicators and a left-hand stalk for a two-speed-plus-intermittent screen wiper. The heater is effective, both in terms of the amount of heat it delivers and where it is delivered, and ventilation can be aided when necessary by the three-speed fan, which is reasonably quiet in operation.

Access to the rear in this hardtop version is limited to a squeeze past the folded-down front seats and, again, entry is encouraged through the passenger door as the seat on that side slides forward as the backrest is flopped down to increase the gap. Early 413 models had a single full-width bench seat in the

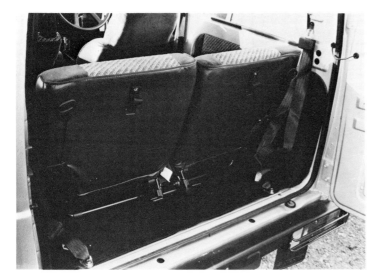

Not much luggage space remains with the rear seats in place, top, but the SJ413V's interior is adaptable. Seats can be folded forward singly, centre, or together, bottom, to increase the load area. The double-fold is achieved by releasing the floor clips at the central bar.

Passenger version of the SJ413V – the JX metal top – has rear windows that hinge open for ventilation, but a bar across to prevent damage to the glass from bulky loads.

rear, designed to flop down flat when the space was needed for luggage rather than passengers. Folding the seat up isn't all that straightforward. To flop the backrest down it is necessary merely to release a pair of catches, but to fold up the base as well two butterfly nuts have to be unscrewed. Though of fairly basic construction, the seat proves reasonably comfortable, with adequate cushion padding and a reasonably high backrest. There is not much room back there; enough headroom and shoulder room for a couple of adults, but short on legroom. And, with the rear seat in position, there is precious little room for luggage. The later Samurai has the same back seat arrangement as the Santana – two quite substantial seats that can be folded up individually, and with a lot less fuss than in earlier models.

Driving the Samurai, it is the greater power of the 1,324cc engine that impresses most. The fact that there's some 40% more power there cuts the acceleration time to 60mph by almost 10sec compared with the SJ410. That's not fast by normal 1,300cc saloon car standards, but is gives the 413 the pep it needs to stay with busy city traffic without being constantly strained to the limit.

Again, it is aerodynamics – or rather the lack of it – that limits the car's top speed, which at 74mph is not all that much of an improvement over the 410. That maximum speed comes up in fourth gear a good 700rpm below its maximum power output speed of 6,000rpm, suggesting that the gearing is too high; with fourth already a mild overdrive it is not surprising that fifth is too high for the car to maintain anything over 70mph on the level. Arguably, a slight lowering of the gearing could add a few mph to the top speed, but as it is, the 413 is at least able to reach and maintain the legal motorway speed limit, with fifth cutting engine noise on level sections enough to make highway cruising more acceptable than in the 410. Not that the 413 is quiet at that speed – even in fifth at 70mph the engine can be heard hard at work, and if the hardtop body improves on the wind noise set up by the vibrating soft-top of the Santana, it serves only to emphasize the roar of the chunky-tread tyres.

The bigger engine doesn't mean heftier controls; the clutch is just as light, the gear lever just as manageable, as on the 410, and the servo-assisted brakes are quite powerful enough to keep the Samurai under control.

For all the improvements to the suspension, the 413 and Samurai still keep the driver alert on the road. The steering is low-geared to take some of the weight out of parking; even so, squeezing the car into a tight space requires quite a lot of muscle. More importantly, though, the low gearing combines with the deadening effect of the hydraulic damper to remove feel and reduce the crispness of steering response. Add to this the fact that a fair amount of axle movement is still allowed to ensure adequate off-road capability, and you'll understand why the 413 – though certainly better than the 410 – still has a tendency to wander a little when running straight, and still displays rather a lot of bump-steer when running over rutted surfaces.

The anti-roll bar on the front does improve matters – a bit. It allows the 413 to be cornered a little faster, so that more use can be made of the engine's better power output, but eventually there is still too much body roll, combined with the same basic tendency to pitch, bounce and hop about, when the car is being hustled along.

Ride comfort is only marginally better. It is not so much a matter of how soft the springs are, more a matter of the difficulty in controlling bounce and rebound in such a light vehicle with springs as primitive as the semi-elliptics used on the SJs, particularly when combined with a short wheelbase that tends to emphasize pitching as well.

Off-road, this car is markedly better than the 410 in several ways. Oddly enough, it is over the rough terrain of cross-country driving that the benefit of the softer suspension can really be felt. It takes the jerk out of many a hump and bump that would have sent a 410 driver bouncing out of the seat.

Naturally, the greater power output allows the car to tackle off-road obstacles with more confidence, but it also allows the driver to practise more in the way of true off-road driving skill, since the broader span of gearing can be used more effectively to match the car's ground speed with the engine's torque band – this is by no means a second-gear-low-ratio-only machine.

The Samurai does have little feelings that show up when the going gets really tricky – the engine's narrow power band means the car can't cope well with really slippery conditions the way an old plodder of a Land Rover can, and the combination of a first gear that isn't really low enough in the low range and the low compression ratio of the engine means there isn't adequate engine braking for easing down a steep slope in gently controlled confidence. The engine is

Centre of the facia provides an extra cubby hole for sunglasses and the like. The digital clock is standard on the later versions.

Substantial bull-bar on this example all but covers the Samurai badges on the front wings. Note the extended wheelarches of the SJ413.

not really gutsy enough to cope with some obstacles in the usual slow-but-sure fashion that is generally considered to be good off-roading practice. At times like these, sheer momentum has to be used to overcome the lack of torque, but the Suzuki has the strength and durability to take as much of that sort of punishment as any owner-driver is likely to hand out.

Even with the 1,324cc engine and the five-speed gearbox, the Suzuki SJ is still relatively slow and noisy. It does have fashionable appeal, though, and as a modish city runabout it has a more lively performance than the 410, enabling it to keep its place quite well in bustling traffic. What is more important, though, is that it is every bit as good as it looks off-road.

Performance – SJ413 Samurai

Maximum speeds		Acceleration from rest		Acceleration in 4th and 5th		
				mph	4th sec	5th sec
5th	71mph	0–30mph	4.6 sec	20–40	10.6	16.2
4th	74mph	0–40	7.5	30–50	11.5	19.0
3rd	64mph	0–50	12.2	40–60	14.6	25.5
2nd	47mph	0–60	19.4	50–70	26.0	–
1st	23mph	0–70	37.3			

Overall fuel consumption – 24.8mpg

Source: *Autocar*, November 25 1987

What to look for

Thinking of buying an SJ secondhand? There are some good ones to be had but a 4x4 needs more than usual care in choosing. Mike Hallett provides a buyer's guide

Many potential owners contemplating a Suzuki SJ will be approaching four-wheel drive motoring for the first time. In this respect the vehicle makes an ideal 'starter pack' as it is relatively cheap, easy to drive,

MIKE HALLETT has been technical editor of *Off Road and 4 Wheel Drive* since it started in 1982. Brought up among Land Rovers on Dartmoor, he has maintained an enthusiasm for go-anywhere vehicles from childhood. Mike was a senior warrant officer in the Royal Electrical and Mechanical Engineers before turning to journalism.

mechanically straightforward and, therefore, simple to both understand and maintain. There is also nothing quite like it for teaching newcomers about the stability of off-road vehicles.

Buying new, of course, avoids any real problems, but many will be looking for used examples and, now that the SJ model has been available for over six years, there is a very wide selection of these available; most appear to have worn rather well. However, don't be deceived by outward appearances. Cute though they may be, Suzukis can hold many of the pitfalls commonly found on any four-wheel drive vehicle; they call for careful scrutiny. The off-road potential of the machine means that it could have suffered severe mechanical abuse without any obvious external signs of it.

Have a look at as many examples as you can before you start getting serious about buying one. This will give you a feel for what is available and the sort of

The SJ is designed for hard use, off the beaten track, but activities such as these make a thorough damage inspection an important part of selecting a used vehicle.

prices they are commanding. Don't rush in and grab the first you see, and don't necessarily go for the 'loaded' example just because it looks the business with all those expensive bolt-on accessories.

Having selected a target vehicle, ask for it to be parked up on level ground so that you can stand back and observe its stance. It must sit level; no odd leaning to front, rear, left or right. Bent axles are not common, but check for them anyway by ensuring the wheels are vertical, and remember, the steering must be set straight ahead when checking the front wheels as the geometry can play tricks when they are angled into a turn.

Look along the body panels for ripples or other evidence of impact damage.

Do this from all directions, as the way the light falls on a panel can reveal many a repair job. It doesn't have to be cause for rejection, but it could show up something nasty and, of course, it helps your negotiations if and when the time comes.

Vehicles that have been used off-road, even competently, will usually show signs of light scratching all over the sides where they have been taken through scrub and heavily overgrown green lanes. This is not important in itself, but an indication that the vendor, or previous owner, has used the vehicle off-road, even if he or she says they haven't. Incidentally, a high proportion of Suzukis are owned by women and although, as a rule, they tend to treat their vehicles better than men do, they are just as prone to being vague, or downright dishonest, about what they got up to with them. No sexual discrimination in this book!

The interior of a Suzuki SJ, particularly the earlier models, is relatively basic: simple plastic facia and lots of bare metal covered by thin, cheap carpet. Many owners will have replaced that with the off-cuts from the new bedroom or hall carpet; if so, it is easy to lift to see if there is any damage to the floor panels caused by heavy off-road abuse. High-mileage vehicles will probably be fairly tatty around the seats and door trim, but this is easily tidied up or replaced.

The Suzuki, as with all off-road vehicles, is likely to have suffered its most telling damage, if any, on the underside. Differential housings hit rocks, cross-members get bent, transfer cases take a hammering from tree stumps and, in extreme cases, even the structure can be distorted.

The ladder-frame chassis, commonly used in four-wheel drive vehicles of all kinds, is a bit of a mixed blessing. It certainly provides the rugged durability required for this type of machine, and helps to keep the centre of gravity down, but it is surprisingly vulnerable to shock damage. A relatively mild front-end shunt which would cause only superficial crumpling on a monocoque car, can easily send a shock wave down a chassis rail that will fracture engine, gearbox and body mountings, or deform outriggers and spring hangers at the opposite end of the vehicle. Secondary damage of this kind isn't always noticed when 'repairs' are implemented and only reveals itself later, usually in the form of an obscure transmission or handling fault. Perhaps surprisingly, few SJs display such damage, not because they are immune – far from it – but because the vast majority of them are never taken over the sort of terrain that inflicts it. Those that are tend to be driven sensibly, but there will always be some around that have been in the hands of a twerp with a disconnected brain. These vehicles may also show signs of having been rolled.

Inspection of the underside is greatly simplified if you can get the prospective purchase up on a ramp or lift, but it is not essential as there is a fair bit of space under a Suzuki for crawling around during the 'poke and prod' session. Look out for the sort of impact damage mentioned above. Most of it

You won't find a used Suzuki with an underbonnet as clean as this sparkling new SJ413, left, but a visual check that everything is tidy and leak-free is vital. So is inspection of panel fits and hinges – for alignment and signs of corrosion.

will have been caused by glancing blows, so is unlikely to be serious. However, large dents in the front of the differential housing, deep gouges in the alloy of the transfer case's lower extremities and/or impact damage inflicted on the drum of the transmission-mounted parking brake, or its backplate, warrant some careful consideration. Not because they are necessarily serious in themselves, but because, as with the chassis, any impact that can cause that sort of apparently superficial damage may have had a more devastating effect on less rugged components further down the line. (By the way, the latest SJ413 models do not feature a transmission brake; their handbrake operates on the rear drums.)

While you are still crawling about underneath, check for fluid leaks from the various gaskets, seals and joints on the engine, differentials, main and transfer gearboxes, steering box and brake and clutch slave cylinders. Look at the hydraulic brake pipes, check that none are damaged or corroded and that the flexible hoses to the front brakes and back axle are serviceable. Check the

With a multi-purpose vehicle such as this, interior condition counts for less than in a conventional car. But check that all standard equipment is present and in working order. Accessory mats, perhaps of the plastic tray type, are useful to protect – or disguise – original floor covering.

wheels and release the handbrake before taking a firm grip on the propeller shafts and turning them back and forth to check for play at the splines and universal joints. Be wary if they turn more than half a revolution. Though most of this will be backlash in the transmission, any more than that is unacceptable. Remember, if freewheel hubs are fitted, the front shaft will merely rotate, which won't help you to establish anything other than the hubs are still unlocked. Engage them when you check the wheels. On earlier models, there could be a problem with excessive and premature wear on the front drive shaft's splines, but this was rectified on later vehicles. Finally, take advantage of the down-under viewpoint to inspect the inner sides of the tyres and wheel rims for signs of abuse – cuts, nicks, bulges, that sort of thing.

If you like what you have seen so far, the next stage, before taking it for a test drive, is to take a look under the bonnet. You are seeking signs of general neglect – perished water hoses, tatty fan belt, bodged wiring, oil and coolant leaks. On some vehicles, this may well turn into quite a prolonged survey –

Rare breed – SJ413 pick-up was a useful workhorse, no longer offered in Britain. Most available secondhand will have been utility, rather than recreational vehicles.

but, by now, you will have more than an inkling of how well the machine has been cared for, so you may not even *want* to drive it. If you are not happy, now is the time to say, 'Thank you and Goodbye', but if there is that rising swell of excitement at the prospect of a 'new' vehicle, have a drive in the thing.

There is not really any advantage to be gained by test-driving a prospective purchase in off-road conditions. It proves little or nothing, and you might just get it bogged in somewhere or even damage it; embarrassing. By all means, slip it into low range – don't forget those freewheel hubs, if fitted – and check that it doesn't leap out of engagement during hard acceleration or on the over-run. Listen for unusual noises; rattles, graunches and knocks are undesirable and quite likely to be expensive to remedy. Avoid too much manoeuvring if you are on a hard, dry surface as you will only wind up the transmission; it is unlikely to do any immediate harm unless something is on the verge of packing up anyway, in which case you will probably help it on its way and create more embarrassment. Generally, though, if the vehicle drives satisfactorily on the road in two-wheel drive, there is no point in hammering it across country as well. Just check that the transfer box performs all its functions without suspicious sound effects. Early SJs with the four-speed primary gearbox

Hot stuff – Allard turbocharged SJ410 has the acceleration of of a 1,600cc saloon, but take care if buying a modified SJ secondhand. Know the extent of the modifications – and remember that faster component wear is likely to accompany higher performance.

occasionally had problems with the synchromesh on third, so check it up and down the ratios.

It doesn't take much of a drive to check out brakes, steering, suspension and general performance, but try to take long enough about it for the engine to get well up to operating temperature. Most units will only reveal their true character when hot and bothered. Try stopping and re-starting it. Look for exhaust smoke when the engine is revved, blue or black, depending on whether it's burning oil or running rich. Listen for odd mechanical noises which may not be apparent until the oil has warmed up a bit, and also listen to the brakes when applied gently. Early Suzukis have drum brakes front and rear, and for a while mud and other foreign bodies could get into them rather too easily. Eventually, shields were introduced which solved this problem. Later models are equipped with disc brakes at the front. If the vehicle you are checking-out has a handbrake mounted on the transfer box output, do not, under any but the most dire circumstances, apply it while the machine is still moving as this doesn't do the transmission any good at all. Handbrake turns are, therefore, not a good idea!

By now you will probably have made your decision. If you are happy that it's a 'good'un', then go for it! If you have any doubts, leave it. There are plenty more Suzukis around to choose from.

Keeping in shape

How to keep your Suzuki 4x4 in top condition and at optimum performance. Mike Hallett advises and gives guidance on tyres and other equipment

One of the problems with off-road four-wheel drive vehicles is that eventually they are used in the sort of conditions for which they were originally designed: scrambling over hillsides, rocks and ruts, slogging through deep mud or loose sand, wading rivers, towing trailers and towing loads.

Sometimes it is absolutely necessary to drive in such places or perform such tasks, but often it is done just for pleasure. Whatever the reason, and however enjoyable one finds it, they are all operating conditions that can cause accelerated wear and tear in any sort of vehicle. The result is that vehicles used in harsh environments need far more loving care and attention if they are to survive the experience for any length of time. All vehicles require thorough periodic servicing and routine maintenance if reliability is to be assured; four-wheel drives just need more of the same.

Possibly, as the proud owner of a Suzuki SJ, you have joined the growing ranks of four-wheel drive enthusiasts for the first time. If you bought your vehicle new or secondhand from a reputable dealer you should not have too many immediate problems as the car will have been serviced and properly prepared for sale. On the other hand, should your supplier have been less than reputable, you could already be discovering just how much effort and expense can go into the upkeep of a 4x4. Wherever you acquired your vehicle, it is generally a good idea to take the time to go over it very thoroughly once you have it on your home ground. It is astonishing how many more blemishes will reveal themselves once the silently accusing vendor is no longer peering over your shoulder.

Although the bodywork is all steel, there does not appear to be any inherent corrosion problems on the SJ range, unlike the earlier LJ models which, when they suffered from the malaise, did so fairly comprehensively. Nevertheless, make the effort to rectify chips and scratches in the paint, as and when they appear, and don't allow rust to become established. However, the principal strength of the vehicle lies in its chassis, so corrosion in the body panels, whilst cosmetically unsightly, isn't likely to result in total physical collapse.

The steering on Suzuki's diminutive off-roader is generally fairly light and

Swivel housings need regular examination for scoring and corrosion. Worn seals mean sloppy steering.

precise, and no power assistance option is available. The system is relatively straightforward and there is not a lot of scope for obscure problems. Damping against road shock or kick-back is partially achieved by use of a hydraulic shock absorber mounted between the Pitman arm (the bit that swings back and forth horizontally under the steering box) and the front cross-member. However, further damping is imposed on the system by the friction of the swivel housing seals. The swivel housings are the big steel 'balls' which house the kingpins and the constant-velocity (C/V) joints at each end of the front axle. Naturally enough, being exposed to water, mud, grit, rock-salt and all the other unmentionables that lurk on or off the road, these seals eventually wear, reducing the amount of damping on the steering. According to the manual, they should be replaced every 6,000 miles, but in reality they tend to be ignored. Consequently, the surface of the swivel housing on which the seal bears and keeps clean becomes progressively more pitted, scratched and corroded. They are not chromium-plated on the Suzuki, as they are on some other 4x4s employing the same idea. Eventually, the seal is worn badly enough for the steering to feel decidely light and for water and other contaminants to find their way into the assembly. Internal lubrication for the kingpins and constant-velocity joint is a slack handful of grease (150g) stuffed in during initial assembly, so there is no oil slopping about in there for the seal to wipe a trace of it over the surface every so often.

The underside of any vehicle, particularly alongside a wheel, is a hostile environment, and when this servicing isn't carried out correctly, the steering is the first system to display symptoms of distress. Other causes of steering wander can be unequal tyre pressures, worn track rod ends, and wear in the steering box or at the Pitman arm splines. The steering box is adjustable to compensate for wear, but it's a tedious business which involves removing the box from the vehicle and measuring the torque taken to start turning the input shaft. Still, the only special 'tools' you need are a piece of string and a spring balance capable of reading up to about 10lb. Wrap the string around the circumference of the flexible rubber coupling, using one of the bolts to anchor it, then hook the other end on to the spring balance. The input shaft should *start* to turn when between 4.5 and 7.5lb are indicated, but never more than that. Adjust and re-check until a figure within this tolerance is attained.

Routine servicing and maintenance on the engine of any 4x4 is much the same as with a conventional vehicle, but some consideration must be given to

Check the cross-member for signs of impact; this one is undamaged.

the effect of off-road operation. Low-ratio work generally means highish engine speeds with low ground speeds, consequently air flow through the radiator isn't always as good as it might be. This doesn't have to be a problem as over-capacity is designed in, but sometimes, often unbeknown to the operator, the matrix or core of the radiator can be partially blocked with mud that has splashed up and subsequently baked on. Consequently, running at high temperatures, if not actually overheating, becomes a definite possibility. After an off-road session or at regular intervals, the matrix should be inspected and, if required, flushed through with clean water from a hose. Soak the mud first to get it soft, then blast it out from behind the radiator, driving it back out the way it came in.

The engine's oil level should obviously be checked fairly frequently, but have an additional quick look before you do any off-roading. The angles that the vehicle can get to during these antics, especially steep descents, means that a low level may cause it to suffer temporary oil starvation at moments of stress, despite the deep, baffled sump pan.

Wading can be a traumatic experience for an unprepared vehicle, but the little Suzuki does quite well on this score. The distributor is mounted on the back of the cylinder head, driven from the end of the overhead camshaft, which puts it well up out of reach of your average water splash. Unless there are faulty ignition leads, there should be no problems of the vehicle shuddering to a halt in these conditions. However, the axle breathers are lightly sprung ball valves screwed into the top of the differential housings with no extension tubes to a higher level. Plunging into water when the axles are nice and warm causes a rapid cooling of the assembly which results in a drop in internal air pressure. A small quantity of water, and whatever else it contains, may then be forced in by atmospheric pressure, not only through the valve, but also past the axle's seals, which easily stop fluid escaping, but can't cope with it trying to get in. Although there is no immediate problem, ignore it at your peril because an emulsion of oil and water does not possess the necessary lubrication qualities for the very high contact pressures generated in a differential. If you've had a day when water and wading was a major feature, check the oil in the final drives when you've finished and replace it if there is any sign of contamination. You'll know it by the creamy, frothy mess that drips out of the drain hole.

One of the major difficulties that many off-road vehicle drivers face is selecting a suitable tyre for their needs. The vehicle's manufacturer, of necessity, always provides what is considered to be a good all-rounder. This will have been thoroughly tested to ensure its compatibility with the vehicle and its characteristics, both on and off the road, before being specified as original equipment (OE) for standard fitment, or even as an option for special conditions. However, the design of most standard OE tyres is heavily biased

Underbonnet layout of the SJ413, above, and SJ410 Santana, below, is similar, though air cleaner arrangements are different. Both have electrics mounted high up for easy access and to keep them as far as possible away from water entering underneath. Wheel jack storage is different in the two models.

Spring shackles and bushes should be checked regularly to ensure that bolts are tight and rubbers in good condition. The front swinging shackle, above, should not have significant sideways movement.

The intermediate shaft between the gearbox and the transfer box is too often a forgotten component, though it is hard to inspect unless you can get the vehicle on to a ramp.

towards on-road performance, which is, after all, where the majority of time is spent, regardless of the fond image we may have of ourselves as inveterate off-roaders.

The design requirements of tyres for different ground conditions vary enormously. Few of us are prepared to cart several sets about in the back of the vehicle and tolerate swapping them around, merely to meet our personal needs, so a tread pattern that is a good compromise is the only way to go if adequate performance is to be achieved irrespective of the terrain to be tackled.

There is a trend amongst some enthusiasts of four-wheel drive vehicles to fit larger than standard tyres on their machines – not only wider, but bigger in diameter, too. They can look good, but be warned: fitting oversize tyres can, and frequently does, introduce other problems, including poor handling, reduced lateral and longitudinal stability, shortened component lives, inferior performance and the potential for problems with both the law (Construction and Use regulations) and insurance companies.

Suzuki originally specified 195SR-15 radial-ply tyres for their SJ range in the UK, though other sizes have been fitted for different markets. It is quite a large tyre for what is, arguably, a small and fairly light car, but it has proved to be a good compromise choice. However, the latest Samurai models are equipped with 205/70SR-15 radials which have a 70 per cent aspect ratio, so are wider, but over half an inch smaller in overall diameter than the earlier type. This, plus the increased track of the newer vehicle, has improved on-road stability considerably. The aspect ratio is the tyre section's height divided by the same section's width, the product being expressed as a percentage. Unless otherwise stated in the tyre size, usually after the section's width in millimetres, the aspect ratio of radials is about 82 per cent. Cross-ply tyres are normally 100 per cent, in other words, their section height and width have approximately the same dimension.

The dilemma facing the Suzuki owner is whether to go for the same sized tyre or perhaps something a little 'meatier'. Bear in mind that wider tyres, though often good and grippy on dry roads, will frequently be unpredictable on wet surfaces, being prone to locking up and sliding because the increase in contact area has effectively reduced the ground pressure and therefore the 'stiction'. It is not recommended that tyres bigger than 215SR-15 are fitted on Suzuki SJs. In the light of the controversy about the stability of four-wheel drive utilities, and Suzukis in particular, it may be as well to opt for a low-profile tyre such as the Samurai's 205/70SR-15 or even a 195/75SR-15, which is slightly taller, but narrower.

In the long run, only the owner really knows what duties the vehicle is most likely to undertake, and where, so tyres should be chosen which best suit this requirement. Remember, an aggressive off-road tread pattern may look the

*Handbrake variations –
on the earlier vehicles a
transmission brake is
used, left, which can be
vulnerable to ground
impact. The SJ413
Samurai models have a
more conventional car
system, with cables to
the rear drum brakes.*

part, but if most of your mileage is on roads, you will find it noisy and uncomfortable. Tyres with a narrower but less aggressive tread will give good handling on the road and perform more than adequately in the rough. If you do find they can't cope on those few occasions when conditions are worse than expected, don't be scared to drop the tyre pressures. This bulges the tread and increases the area in contact with the ground, giving improved 'flotation' and traction. However, do not lower the pressure too far as you could inadvertently dislodge the tyre bead from its seat, losing what little air is left. On a Suzuki, about 12psi is the absolute minimum, but drive very gingerly at that. Inflate to the regular 20psi or so as soon as possible – and certainly before venturing back on to tarmac.

Despite appearances and its lightweight construction, a Suzuki SJ is a tough little character, but it is not unbreakable. Off-road driving imposes high torsional loads on chassis and body alike, and a few miles of rough tracks can take more out of the axles, springs and various attachment points than hundreds of miles of sealed main road surface.

On the road, never forget that it is an off-road utility vehicle at heart. It has a high centre of gravity, a short wheelbase, high ground clearance, firm springs and a wheel at each corner – all characteristics that enhance its off-road ability, but do little for on-road handling. It makes demands of driving skills not required to the same degree by more conventional machines. So be gentle with it, treat it with respect, and it will serve you well.

Alloy wheels and big tyres look smart – but may not drive as well as the standard fitments.

MORE THAN JUST MUSCLE

ON SALE EVERY MONTH

Added values

There are lots of tempting accessories available for the SJ. John Beese reviews what's available, from the really useful to the purely cosmetic

JOHN BEESE is the Editor of *Off Road and 4 Wheel Drive*, Britain's premier magazine dealing with four-wheel drive vehicles. A great off-road motoring enthusiast, he first became interested in such vehicles when writing about quarrying for a mining industry journal.

Set for the beach — Suzuki equipped this SJ410 for the windsurfing set, including suitable side graphics.

W hen a car becomes fashionable the vehicle accessories market
wastes no time in responding. The Suzuki SJ series of four-wheel
drive vehicles has had a growing cult image since its launch in
1982. A car that was originally designed to sell in third world countries with
tough, reliable, easy-to-maintain components and excellent off-road
characteristics has captured the imagination of western world car enthusiasts
and resulted in a super smart-looking machine with rugged appeal.

Not everyone buys an SJ just for its looks. Suzuki estimate that 20% of their
SJ vehicle sales are to people who genuinely need the off-road capabilities to

access difficult areas; 60% of owners cited the four-wheel drive ability as being a major factor in their vehicle choice. Of course, many people choose the SJ as a value-for-money second car with the ability to cope with a difficult winter. The SJs market is a wide one and it is this fact that accounts for the vast array of bolt-on goodies available. Suzuki's official accessories list alone includes well over 70 items!

Many of the lines colourfully displayed in glossy brochures such as inclinometers, free-wheeling hubs, side rails, bull bars and even altimeters will present many new SJ owners with a new language they don't understand. Too often the person selling such gimmicks won't know much, either. This chapter is designed to make sure you *do* enjoy the benefits of any accessories you decide to buy.

Bull bars or 'roo bars: Most people who purchase a bull bar for the front of their vehicle are doing so to enhance the overall appearance of the machine. Very few people in Europe have a practical need for such a device. The idea came from Australia, where vehicles driving in remote regions at night

SJ413V JX featuring surf/ski bar set, luggage rack, wrap-round bull bar with grille, side sill step set and Hella halogen driving lamps – all from Suzuki's accessory range.

frequently hit kangaroos mesmerized by the vehicle's headlights, causing severe damage. This led to the development of extra protection to the front of the vehicle in the form of welded metal tubes that became known as 'roo bars and eventually to the rest of the world as bull bars. Bull bars do give added protection against minor traffic accidents but most are difficult to repair once damaged and in a more serious shunt can be bent into the bodywork, causing damage that might otherwise have been absorbed by the standard, relatively cheap-to-replace bumper. Bars that wrap around the front sides of the vehicle are particularly vulnerable to this. If you are buying a bull bar for visual reasons it is best to choose a lightweight aluminium version as this will wear well and not create too much unnecessary weight over the front wheels. Prices start at around £100 for the most basic models.

Side sills: Side sills, whether in the form of a step or straight bar positioned below the doors, parallel to the vehicle, have little practical use. For serious off-road work they can be a positive nuisance as they are vulnerable to being damaged or even stopping the vehicle when driving over a steep-sided mound. If the side rails are strong enough the vehicle can be left pivoting on the side rails with all four wheels clear of the ground – this is known as being 'high-centred'. In this situation, poorly made side rails are likely to become bent into the bodywork of the car, causing expensive damage. However, most people don't demand this level of off-road ability from their Suzuki, and side steps can be a real bonus in helping elderly or disabled people climb in and out of the vehicle. Prices start at around £80 a pair.

Light grilles: There are several styles of light protector grilles available to fit over the headlights, rear lights and even side indicators and they can afford some protection. If you intend driving your vehicle through dense undergrowth where it is likely to come into contact with heavy branches, then such grilles are probably a good idea. For town use they are mainly purchased for visual enhancement and they can look very smart, but remember that in most cases a damaged grille is more expensive to replace than a light lens. Most grilles are held in place by self-tapping screws and if this job isn't properly finished you can find them becoming a rust trap. Prices start at around £30 for a complete set of guards.

Altimeter/inclinometer: Whether purchased separately or as part of a set, altimeters and inclinometers fitted in four-wheel drive vehicles score a good many poser points, but have no practical use. If you have the vehicle tipped at a critical angle – for the Suzuki, around 50 degrees, depending on your speed and surface conditions – you certainly won't be in the position to examine a tilt meter; all your concentration will be taken with the task of finding more level ground. Altimeters, if they are accurate, give you an indication of your height above sea level, but then so does a good map. And if you are driving at the sort of altitude that could cause your normally-aspirated Suzuki to lose power through lack of oxygen, there's not much you can do practically about it anyway. Having said that, the added instrumentation can do much to enhance the appearance of the dashboard. Suzuki quote a price of £130 for their Altimeter/Inclinometer set.

Body kits: Oasis 4x4 Designer Accessories produce a body kit that widens the profile of the SJ, giving it a more squat appearance. Predominantly made of glass-fibre, the entire kit, including widened bumper/spoilers, costs just under £650, excluding fitting. If nothing else, this kit will make your Suzuki stand out from the crowd.

Wider wheels: Fitting wider, chunky-looking wheels and tyres to four-wheel drives undoubtedly gives such vehicles a more macho appeal and has proved particularly popular with people in countries such as the US, Canada and Australia. If the tyres are significantly wider than the standard equipment, then vehicle lifting kits and axle spacers are often required to lift the body clear of the tyres to allow the front wheels enough travel to steer sufficiently. As we discuss in Chapter 6, such a modification can seriously alter the handling geometery of your Suzuki, making the vehicle less stable and increasing drive-line wear. The road handling of the vehicle will not be as good as the standard machine and when being used off-road the only occasion when such wheels and tyres would prove an advantage is when crossing boggy ground, where the wide tyres would increase the vehicle's flotation characteristics. Suzuki recommend that you do not make such a modification, but if you are determined to go ahead with such a scheme check to see how it affects your vehicle warranty and insurance. Some people choose to fit low-profile tyres on the vehicle's standard rims to give a chunkier-looking wheel. No problem here, but it can reduce the rolling radius of the wheels, which means that the speedometer/mileometer will need recalibrating.

Finishing touches: Most of the companies listed at the end of this chapter offer trim kits consisting of specialy designed stick-on graphics suitable for bodywork and wheels, and the best way to make your choice is to request brochures from each. Suzuki's 'Approved Accessories' booklet has the most comprehensive range.

Thus far, we have dealt with items that are primarily cosmetic. The list of SJ fitments that present practical advantages is a long one and some of the more specialized accessories need only a cursory mention here.

An altimeter and an inclinometer fit neatly into the centre of the SJ413's facia. Fun to have, but they are not as useful for off-roading as they might seem.

Spare wheel cover with Suzuki GB's classic rhino symbol. Several alternative designs are available.

Standard bull-bar set without the wrap-round shown on page 80. This one is suitable for both SJ410 and SJ413.

Suzuki's sports steering wheel fitted to an SJ410, which also has an inclinometer fitted in the central circular 'blank' and a supplementary instrument pod on top of the dashboard.

If you are the hunting type, the Suzuki catalogue offers a selection of smart dog guards, separating the rear compartment from the front seats, on to which you can fit gun clips. Suzuki quote a price of £80 for a dog guard and a set of gun clips cost around £19.

For the surfboard/skiing enthusiast, Suzuki offer a smart, specially designed roof rack for £175.

The standard driving lights fitted to the SJ range are perfectly adequate, but many companies make fog lights and spot lights suitable for the vehicle. The Suzuki-approved, Hella halogen items cost £46 and are designed to fit easily on to Suzuki's own bull bars.

Spare wheel covers with the Suzuki Rhino motif must be one of the most distinguishing features of the vehicle. These are available in a wide variety of designs including a fair selection depicting over-friendly rhinoceri. The Suzuki owner with a total disregard for common decency can even buy mud flaps to match.

Roll bar: This £90 (Suzuki-recommended) item is a worthwhile investment for additional roll-over protection. Like all serious off-road vehicles, the SJ range of jeeps has a relatively high centre of gravity and, should it be involved in an

Full roll-over bar for soft-top SJs also serves as an attachment for dog guard – both are Suzuki-approved.

Freewheeling hubs make for smoother, more efficient running on the road, but each needs to be locked manually when four-wheel drive is engaged.

accident or driven recklessly, is more likely to land on its roof than a roadgoing car. The Suzuki-recommended roll bar is designed for the soft-top SJ where the standard vehicle is protected only by a box-section metal frame, which may not be really adequate in a high-speed accident.

Freewheeling hubs: The four-wheel drive system on the SJ range is part-time, allowing two-wheel drive for normal road use and four-wheel drive for slippery conditions or off-road work. This is selected by the driver via the secondary gear stick, or 'transfer lever'. The problem, on models fitted without freewheeling hubs, is that when the vehicle is in two-wheel drive (driving through the rear prop-shaft only) the front wheels push the front-drive shafts, differential and prop-shaft round, using more power and therefore petrol than necessary. Freewheeling hubs get round this problem by allowing the front wheels to rotate freely when the car is in two-wheel drive, leaving the front drive-line stationary. The hubs recommended by Suzuki retail at just under £100. The disadvantages, apart from finding the money, are that you need to manually engage the hubs at the wheel before you are able to engage four-wheel drive via the transfer lever. For £256 automatic freewheeling hubs are available which do not need to be manually engaged and are disconnected by simply reversing the vehicle a few yards.

Several firms offer hardtops for open SJs – this one, shown on an Allard turbocharged SJ413, is part of an American-manufactured body kit from Oasis.

Hardtops: Oasis accessories and Suzuki's own accessories catalogue feature hardtops designed to fit soft-top versions of the SJ jeep. If you have enough storage room to keep the glass-fibre top when not in use, this can give you the option of open-top motoring in the summer and a cosy, quiet ride in cold weather. Suzuki's deluxe hardtop retails at around £750 and includes side windows, rear window and sunroof.

Other sensible ideas: A locking handbrake is available from Suzuki, price £30, and is recommended for fitment to the soft-top vehicle vulnerably parked in the street. Locking wheel nuts, £26 per set, can save your wheels in a similar situation, whilst plastic tray foot mats (£25) can prevent your muddy boots dirtying the inside of your vehicle. You will be popular in snowy conditions when you can show off by towing everyone else out of trouble, but a tow ball set, at around £70, will make this easier and, of course, enable you to tow trailers – in the SJ413's case, braked trailers up to 1,100kg.

We have looked at the considerations in tyre type in Chapter 6, but even when you have decided what is best for your needs, the variety of tyres available for off-road vehicles is bewildering – as is the range of prices quoted for the same make at different retail outlets around the country. Many tyre

For a working vehicle a plastic protector – a large moulded tray fitting the rear load compartment, is a good way of keeping the interior clean and undamaged. Towing kit from Suzuki includes the bar itself, brackets, attachments and all the necessary electrics.

salesmen and adverts will try to tell you their tyres cope with everything, but this simply isn't true. You can broadly group tyres in this market into three categories; roadgoing, mud-and-snow pattern, and off-road. A tyre designed for road use only will severely restrict the performance of your vehicle off-road, but can be good at tackling powder snow. Mud-and-snow patterns are the nearest thing to compromise off-road, on-road tyres and are recommended for normal vehicle use. Knobbly tyres with lots of grip in muddy conditions will be noisy and wear badly on the road as well as providing poor grip on bends. The emphasis of the various designs by companies such as BF Goodrich, Firestone, Dunlop, Michelin, Mickey Thompson, Armstrong, and so on, varies considerably and a good source of comparison are the tyre tests undertaken by *Off Road and 4 Wheel Drive* magazine. Shop around for the best prices.

Off-road tackle: If you go off-road and get stuck and there is no-one around to pull you out, you will need some self-recovery tackle. The most basic gear consists of a good spade, rope and vehicle jack; if you know how, these can get you out of most situations. For the more severely bogged SJ driver, a number of hand-operated winches exist that can help pull you out; prices for these start at around £90. You can buy a front-mounted, 4,500lb-capacity, electrically operated winch from Bushey Hall Winches & Equipment Ltd for around £400, but you will probably also need the fitting kit, priced at £135, which includes an above-bumper mounting kit, bull bar and isolator switch. This winch would also suit the boat owner who needs to raise and lower his craft into the water. Ryders International also offer a range of winches suitable for the SJ.

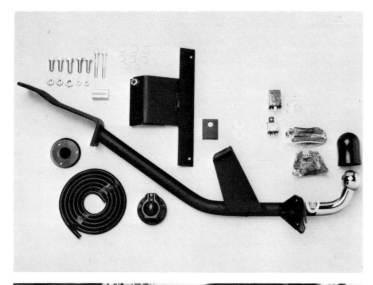

A Spax adjustable shock absorber on a test rig. Fitting such dampers can greatly improve the SJ's on-road ride quality.

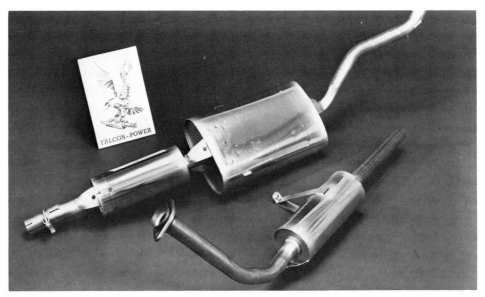

This stainless steel exhaust system from Oasis has a freer flow than the standard item and is claimed to add 10% to power output.

Shock tactics: One of the biggest drawbacks of using an SJ for everyday road work is its bumpy ride. Some people see the rapid pitching motion and jolting as part of the fun – but others don't and would like it improved. Fundamental modifications to the suspension system are impractical, but the ride quality can be improved by fitting more sophisticated shock absorbers than those supplied with the vehicle. Gas-filled shock absorbers are manufactured by Monroe and Rancho and are available in the UK, whilst Spax shock absorbers, of Bicester, produce an excellent adjustable model suitable for the Suzuki. Prices start at around £100 a set. *Off Road and 4 Wheel Drive* have tested all three examples on SJ models and recommend them. Shop around for the best deal.

Hotting up: If you are more accustomed to the performance of a hot hatchback, the 45bhp SJ410 might seem a bit gutless, and although the 1.3-litre SJ413 has considerably better acceleration than its stablemate, road performance is still modest. The dilemma is that these cars were never designed to be high-performance road cars and don't have the road handling to cope with speed. But if you are determined to instill more life into the engine, the two most notable companies offering conversions are Allard Turbomaster and Janspeed Engineering. Allard do a very good job of fitting a Garrett T2 turbocharger into the SJ. The complete package costs around £1,000 and makes the 970cc SJ410 accelerate more like a 1,600cc car. Janspeed don't offer a turbo conversion, but a performance kit for both the SJ410 and 413. Stage One features a Weber carburettor and an extractor exhaust system, producing a claimed increase in power of 24bhp on the SJ410's 970cc motor. The complete Stage One package costs around £690 fitted. Suzuki warn that this kind of engine modification invalidates the vehicles warranty.

Janspeed Stage 1 conversion gives a 24bhp power boost and makes the SJ413 pretty lively. Remember, though, that engine modifications such as this can invalidate the vehicle warranty.

Making contact:

Accessory companies
SUZUKI GB CARS official catalogue:
46-62 Gatwick Road, Crawley, West Sussex, RH10 2XF.
Tel: 0293 518000 (plus all official dealers).
OASIS 4X4 DESIGNER ACCESSORIES, Oasis House, Barfreston, Dover, CT15 7JH.
Tel: 0304 831685.
SILVER KNIGHT SALES, 291 Sovereign Road, Kings Norton, Birmingham, B30 13H.
Tel: 021 451 3911.
AUTOLOOKS UK LTD, 41 Bromwich Road, Woodseats, Sheffield, S80 GG.
TRAILBLAZER, 224 Ashby Road, Shepshed, Loughborough, Leicestershire, LE12 9EF.
Tel: 0509 502226.

Shock absorber suppliers
BILSTEIN, Magard Ltd, 327 East Park Road, Leicester, LE5 5AY.
Tel: 0533 730831.
RANCHO, Trans-Atlantic 4x4 UK Ltd, The Willows, Lodge Lane, Kirby-la-Ashfield, Notts.
Tel: 0623 755564.
SPAX Ltd, Bicester, Oxon.
Tel: 0869 244771.
MONROE AUTO EQUIPMENT Ltd, Rosemary House, Lanwades Business Park, Kennet, Newmarket, Suffolk.
Tel: 0638 751633.

Engine modification companies
ALLARD TURBOMASTER LTD, Unit 4, Crucible Court, Mishet Industrial Park, Coleford, Gloucestershire, GL16 8RE.
Tel: 0594 36227.
JANSPEED ENGINEERING, Castle Road, Salisbury, Wiltshire.
Tel: 0722 21833.

Winches
BUSHEY HALL WINCHES, Unit 7, Lismirrane Industrial Park, Elstree Road, Elstree, Borehamwood, Herts, WD6 3EE.
Tel: 01 953 6050.
RYDERS INTERNATIONAL, Winch Division, 215 Knowsley Road, Bootle, Liverpool, L20 4NW.
Tel: 051 922 7585.

Taking to the rough

For many, owning an SJ is an introduction to an adventurous new hobby – driving off-road. Nigel Fryatt explains how and where to do it

I f you want to go off-roading, you've already made one important decision, and that is to buy Suzuki. It would be wrong to claim that the Suzuki SJ is the king of all off-roaders but, driven correctly, it can hold its head up high. The vehicle has been winning many friends among the hardened off-roading fraternity since it first arrived in the UK in 1982.

The Suzuki SJ has a lot going for it when it comes to the tricky stuff; it is light and has a wheel 'at each corner', with very little front or rear overhang. So, what are we waiting for? Let's go off-road....

Hang on, it's not quite that simple. There are a few golden rules without which you could find yourself in trouble. The first rule is that off-roading is completely different from driving a 'normal' car on tarmac. Different, but not difficult. Ignore any of those people who shake their heads, take a sharp intake of breath and tell you that this is not something for the novice. Off-roading is for everybody and if you do it properly you will enjoy it.

It makes a lot of sense to watch others driving off-road first. As a Suzuki owner, you have the facilities of the Rhino Club at hand and that might be the best place to start. However, you certainly don't need to wait if there isn't a Club meeting planned or you live a long way away. Check for the locations of off-road competitions detailed in Chapter 9 and have a look at how the others do it. If your first impression is one of awe, don't be dismayed. Take my word for it, learning the ropes is easy.

Make sure you know your vehicle. That may sound obvious, but you might be surprised how many drivers don't – presumably the great rush of enthusiasm clouds the judgment. One recent winter, for instance, I came across a Suzuki driver struggling to get his SJ out of a snowy car park.

NIGEL FRYATT was Editor of *Off Road and 4 Wheel Drive* but in 1988 was appointed to the editorship of the Link House motoring flagship *Cars and Car Conversions*. A veteran of the Camel Trophy and other off-road events, he retains a strong interest in 4x4 vehicles. Nigel is the author of MRP's Off Road and 4 Wheel Drive Handbook.

Wandering over to see what the trouble was, the spinning rear wheels and stationary fronts said it all. He'd forgotten to lock the free-wheeling front hubs. Shifting the transfer box lever into low-ratio four-wheel drive won't do anything if the front hubs are not locked. If they are fitted to your Suzuki, always remember to lock them first.

Have a look at the ground clearance under your vehicle. Make a mental note of the position of the differentials so you can try to avoid smashing them against any rocks or tree stumps – not always possible, but worth thinking about.

One rule that is similar to car driving relates to seat belts. If you go off-road on private land, wearing seat belts is not a legal requirement, but it is a must – for you and your passengers.

It is going to get bumpy out there, so sit tight. Remind your passengers to keep their hands inside the vehicle, especially if you have a soft-top Suzuki. Get them to hold on to something so that, in the unlikely event of you rolling over, there will be no flailing arms to become injured.

As the driver, you will have a steering wheel to grab on to, of course, but when you go off-road, *don't* hold on too tight. When you drive off-road, that wheel will have a mind of its own. As the front wheels hit bumps, rocks and ruts, the steering wheel will jerk violently at times. For that very reason, keep your thumbs on top of the rim, not hooked on to a spoke. You will only forget to do it once, but if you have one of those smart sports wheels on your Suzuki, the metal spokes could break a thumb, so watch out! The Suzuki SJ does, in fact, have very good steering for off-roading as it is bushed and damped to insulate the driver from the worst jolts. (It is this damping that makes the Suzuki's steering feel a little imprecise when on the road.)

Off-road, you slot the Suzuki's stubby little auxiliary gear lever into low-ratio four-wheel drive. Once you have changed into low range you use the regular gear lever in the normal way. Low range increases the torque to the Suzuki's wheels and this will allow you to drive much more slowly without slipping the clutch. That is important. You must never slip the clutch off-road. Think of the clutch pedal as a switch, either in or out. If you slip it you are probably in the wrong gear and very likely about to find yourself in trouble.

The main rule to remember is 'take it easy'. If you think off-roading is all about thrashing around, spinning wheels and throwing mud and rocks everywhere, you are wrong. A good off-road driver has a very sensitive right foot, knowing exactly how much power needs to be applied and when it needs applying. It varies for different vehicles, but it is fair to say that with a Suzuki you will need to keep the engine singing. The little Japanese power unit has a big heart, but it is a little low in the torque stakes, so you have to drive accordingly.

Good off-roaders are driving 10 or 15 yards ahead, always watching what is coming up. This may mean that occasionally you have to stop and get out.

Glorious mud – driving your Suzuki in conditions like these, which would defeat any ordinary car, is part of the fun of ownership. But before you venture off-road, learn the basic rules and techniques, says author Nigel Fryatt.

While this may not sound too macho, it is the right way to do it, especially in a Suzuki. If there is a particularly nasty gradient ahead of you, then you will need a certain amount of momentum to get you through, whereas a bigger-engined off-roader could plod through at a snail's pace. Extra momentum will take you where a lack of low-down torque and traction fails, but it is important to note this does not mean flat-out in fifth. Second gear is the most used ratio off-road, even for pulling away. In most instances you'll spend much of your time using second and third gears.

Together with that sensitive right foot, you need smooth, flowing movements of the steering wheel. Yank the wheel one way or another in muddy conditions and the vehicle will simply plough straight on in terminal understeer.

Sometimes, the gearbox can slow the vehicle down better than the brakes. Heavy use of the brake pedal may just lock everything up. Often, a much better way of doing it is to change down a gear to make the wheels turn slower. That is never better displayed than when going downhill.

In my view, there is nothing better than driving *down* a steep, slippery slope. This is what most impresses inexperienced passengers, too.

Before you do go down any slope, get out and have a look. Sitting behind the wheel at the top, you won't be able to see a lot until it is too late, so look before you leap. Then it is a case of engaging low-ratio first gear, drive the vehicle

Going strong – an LJ80 makes easy work of a steep and awkward quarry rise.

over the edge, and then make sure your feet are off *all* the pedals. That may seem a little difficult at first, but it is the right way. Let the vehicle do the work, and *never* declutch going down a slope. If you do, you'll have no control whatsoever and stamping on the brakes is unlikely to help; with all the wheels locked up, you will simply toboggan down. The Suzuki will not steer very well like that, either, so we could be talking about dented panels and unnecessary repair bills.

With your feet well off the pedals, the engine braking will be enough in most cases to get you safely down. Gentle braking is possible if you think it is all happening a little too quickly, but make sure you don't lock the wheels. It could be that as you go down you feel the rear end stepping out of line a little, the back seemingly travelling faster than the front. If this happens, you need to have a few more revs and so you should accelerate a touch. That is a lot easier to write than do for the first time, but it does work.

Going up a hill in a Suzuki needs a little more enthusiasm of the right foot. As I have explained, steep gradients can defeat the Suzuki unless your ascent is well-planned. Second gear, possibly even third, and a decent amount of momentum will see the little machine climb most things. At the very top,

This Santana driver shows how not to do it – he is approaching a tricky descent at an angle, rather than square-on, and thus puts himself at risk of rolling over.

Not so much off-road as on-river! This lady's SJ410 negotiates a rocky river bed. Cool as a mountain stream. . .

always lift off the accelerator so that you slow, or even stop, at the summit. You won't have been able to see what comes next and you will not want to charge up the slope with your front wheels rearing up in the air at the top; that is when the damage is done.

You are only really likely to have problems if you stop halfway up a slope. Don't panic – this is not a problem if you know what you are doing.

If you do stop on a slope because the wheels have started to spin or the engine has cried 'enough', wait until the vehicle is stationary before applying the handbrake. On most Suzukis this works on the transmission so it must not be applied while the vehicle is in motion. Once stationary, you can assess the situation. Never try to turn round or traverse a steep slope. All slopes should be approached square-on wherever possible and climbed straight up, not at an angle. If you try to turn round and have the vehicle sideways-on, you are risking it rolling over. If you have one of those inclinometers in your Suzuki, never let the sideways tilt angle get near 30 degrees; that figure does rest on the side of caution, but if you exceed it once and try again it could spell disaster because the conditions of two slopes will never be the same, even if the angle of the slope is.

You can always come back down the way you went, in reverse. The low-ratio gears work on reverse, so you can do a rather clever and simple backwards hill start. If you have let the vehicle stall to a halt before engaging the handbrake, slip the Suzuki into reverse, then, with your feet off the pedals, turn on the ignition and release the handbrake at the same time. The Suzuki should then happily and slowly chug backwards down the slope to where you can have another go.

Once you have driven up and down a few muddy slopes, got stuck, reversed, tried again and succeeded, you will have done the ground work to become a good off-roader. Crossing rutted muddy ground, remember that advice to know your ground clearance. The Suzuki is a light, reasonably small vehicle, so take care following ruts. If the ruts were cut by a lumbering great Land Rover they may be too deep for you, and your Suzuki will bottom out on the ridge in the middle, with all four wheels spinning aimlessly. Think about straddling the ruts if possible, or just keep two wheels in the ruts and the other two on higher ground.

Remember, too, when crossing ruts or deep grooves in the ground to do so at an angle; *don't* stick both front wheels in the rut at the same time. The axle articulation of the Suzuki is somewhat restricted due to its live axle/leaf spring suspension set-up, but it will cope with some very severe terrain if driven properly.

Driving off-road in the UK is likely to be in mud. There are a lot of different varieties of mud and the important thing is to check that the tyres you have are good at self-cleaning; this is a tyre's ability to rid itself of the mud that gets stuck in the tread. If your tyres are worn, this will be decreased. Off-roaders don't get far on bald tyres.

Keep your eyes peeled for rocks and tree stumps as they can be very damaging to the underside of the vehicle. After an off-road session always have a look underneath to see if there are any tell-tale oil leaks or nasty dents in your sump guard. It is worth washing under here with a high-pressure hose to ensure

Taking to the water if fun, but beginners tend to approach too fast with the danger of both the vehicle's electrics and passengers getting soaked. A pool of water should be inspected for depth before entering.

Cresting the rise – because its power and torque are limited, an SJ needs a burst of throttle to see it up steep climbs, but properly driven it will go almost anywhere.

everything is in good working order for next time.

Sand is one of the most difficult surfaces. In the UK, sand driving is likely to be on a beach and a number of off-roaders have got stuck and had to watch the tide come in and ruin their beloved machines. If you are going to drive on sand, lower your tyre pressures to allow the weight of the vehicle to be spread further (proper sand tyres can be purchased that do the job much better than standard off-road 'nobblies'). Steady and constant is the way; too much right foot and wheelspin could bury your vehicle and, if you stop, it may not be possible to get started again. Sand is not a good medium for the real beginner. If you plan to drive on sand near the sea, take an experienced guide or, at the very least, check the tides!

Snow and ice are more usual conditions in the UK. This is when you will be glad to have four-wheel drive, but remember that the laws of physics still apply; you may have the traction to get going, but a slippery road surface will still make stopping a problem.

Water is an altogether different proposition, but a good example of just how much good fun four-wheel drives are. Your Suzuki will take you through some very wet conditions with ease. But the trick with pools of water is to know what the bottom is like. If you can't, or don't want to wade into a potential river crossing to feel the firmness of the bottom, then grab a long stick and have a good poke about. But don't just prod about aimlessly – see if there are any underwater wheel tracks which could indicate a deeper spot. If it is firm enough, then in you go.

Steep drops into water need to be taken like most slopes – in first gear, Low ratio – but when you are level it may make sense to snatch second to have a little more speed through. Don't go flying into the water, but do use enough speed to create a good wave in front of the vehicle and keep the speed up to keep that bow wave going.

If you have read all this and can't wait to have a go, please don't just drive out into the country and turn off the main road down the first muddy track you can find. 'Green laning' is a real pleasure for the off-roader, but here we don't just have golden driving rules, we also have legal ones.

There is no simple, legal definition of a green lane or green road, so don't think you will find them marked on an Ordnance Survey map. What you need are tracks that have vehicular Rights of Way, but just because somewhere has tyre tracks on it does not mean you can follow. All Rights of Way information is held on definitive maps at the respective highway authorities – and you do have a right to ask to look at them. If you go down to your local County Council offices you are looking for RUPPs – Roads Used as Public Paths. But take care, not all RUPP have vehicular rights. If you find a BOAT, this is more promising because these are Byways Open to All Traffic, but it is possible for a BOAT to have a Traffic Regulation Order restricting vehicular rights.

Going down a slippery slope needs engine, rather than wheel braking. Engage low-ratio first gear, and take your feet off all the pedals until you are back on more even ground.

You may feel that all this is a bit too much bureaucracy and red tape. Well, don't loose heart. Contact your local four-wheel drive club (these are listed in the monthly magazine *Off Road and 4 Wheel Drive*) and see if they have a Rights of Way officer. Most clubs have such a post and these people often get to know the best green lanes in the area as well as the Council officers who are prepared to help.

In most cases it pays to join the local club, if only to find out about green laning and being able to join organized groups. You should never go green laning alone, anyway – two's both company and much safer should you get stuck or break down.

There is a certain amount of the Boy Scout ethic in good green laning. By that I mean 'Be Prepared'. Essential items that you should always carry are a shovel, a strong tow rope, a substantial jack and a First Aid Kit. You will get stuck when driving off-road at some time or other, so the shovel and rope are sure to get used, and the First Aid Kit is sensible because of the rural nature of the drive.

Remember, while you are green laning, that other people use the same tracks, especially ramblers and horse riders. Some hooligan off-roaders give the sensible majority a bad name, so don't race and always stop and allow walkers and horses to go past. Take care not to destroy the tracks or the vegetation. If you are challenged, but you know that the route has vehicular Rights of Way, be polite but firm. There are many pressure groups trying to stop any form of green laning for four-wheel drives, so don't give them ammunition to the cause. There are an estimated 120,000 miles of non-metalled tracks across the UK, but many are under threat. Be sensible, and we can all enjoy green laning.

One way of making sure you get in no-one's bad books is to go to an off-road school. You can learn more about off-road driving, gain some instruction and have fun with other like-minded people.

A number of off-road schools have sprung up over the last year or so and the ones listed at the end of this article are known to the author – this is an observation, not necessarily a recommendation! Check that what they have on offer suits you. Do you want to use your own four-wheel drive, or do you feel safer in one belonging to the school? Do you want instruction on all aspects of off-roading – driving, winching, recovery techniques – or are you looking for an off-road safari where you are driven? There is no official organization to oversee driver instruction, so it can vary from school to school. The best advice is to talk to other members of the Rhino Club to see what they think. Like lots of things, personal recommendation is the best advice.

Whatever route you choose, I am sure you will enjoy off-roading your Suzuki. A neat, simple design that's easy to drive, it makes a great off-roader and you will find that a Suzuki's small size is often an advantage, allowing you to find a way through that other, heavier, off-roaders can't manage.

Oops! A trials-prepared Suzuki complete with full roll-cage takes a tumble during an All-Wheel Drive Club event. Competitive off-road driving is a quite different proposition to green-laning, as the next chapter explains.

OFF-ROAD DRIVING SCHOOLS

Rough Terrain Training Centre
36 Hinton Road, Woodford Halse, Daventry, Northants.
Tel: 0327 61886. Ask for Peter Clifford.

Motor Safari
42 Hoole Road, Hoole, Chester CH2 3NL.
Tel: 0244 548849. Ask for Peter Morgan.

The Overlander Off-Road Centre
East Foldhay, Zeal Monachorum, Crediton, Devon EX17 6DH.
Tel: 036 33 666. Ask for David Bowyer.

Ronnie Dale Off-Road Adventure Driving School
Whiteburn, Abbey St Bathans, Duns, Berwickshire TD11 3RU.
Tel: 03614 244/233. Ask for Ronnie Dale.

Northern Safaris
121 Goodshaw Lane, Goodshaw, Rossendale, Lancashire BB4 8DJ.
Tel: 0706 227456. Ask for Bill Jones.

Highland Drovers
Croft of Kincardine, Boat of Garten, Inverness-shire PH24 3BY.
Tel: 047 983 329. Ask for Frank Spencer or Graham Clark.

Sweetwoods Off-Road Centre
Sweetwoods, Cowden, Edenbridge, Kent TN8 7JN.
Tel: 034286 729. Ask for Peter or Jennifer Strand.

Warwickshire College of Agriculture
Moreton Morrell, Warwick CV35 9BL.
Tel: 0926 651367.

Getting together

The Rhino Club is a great way to meet fellow Suzuki 4x4 enthusiasts and start off-road competition. Appetite whetted, more serious events are available in Britain and abroad, as Bob Cooke explains

There is an irony in that four-wheel drive vehicles that encourage getting away from it all also bring a camaraderie. Off-road enthusiasts like to get together and a variety of clubs exist to foster their interest. That these clubs are so well supported is partly because of the difficulties for individuals in finding suitable, problem-free areas on which to exercise their vehicles. As the previous chapter points out, simply establishing entitlement to use a green lane can be a complicated business.

Some of the best places for off-road driving are disused quarries and Ministry of Defence properties that are used for testing tanks and armoured personnel carriers. A recognized club can obtain permission to use such areas when an individual could not. It is an easy step from that to some kind of organized competitive activity. Those of interest to most Suzuki owners are 'non-damaging' RTV (Road Taxed Vehicle) Trials, and by far the best opportunity to start those is through the Rhino Club.

The Rhino Club is run by the British importers of Suzuki vehicles, Suzuki Cars GB Ltd, and membership is free to anyone owning a Suzuki 4x4, new or secondhand. It was started six years ago to cultivate a feeling of 'belonging' among the expanding group of Suzuki owners of Suzuki owners and now has over 5,000 registered members and attracts up to 500 vehicles to its regular cross-country events.

There is a good family atmosphere at Rhino Club rallies. What started as a British initiative has spread to other countries and the Club's major event held in May now attracts a sizable number of overseas visitors. Through the Club's regular magazine *Rhino News* there is also a friendly link with Suzuki owners' clubs further afield, like the Suzuki 4WD Club of Australia and the Jimny Club of Japan.

In general, the areas picked by the Rhino Club for their regular meetings are sites used by the All-Wheel Drive Club for trials and off-road races, and the terrain includes much more in the way of testing obstacles than mere rocky tracks or muddy patches. There are usually precipitous long drops into deep

Somewhere in the forest... Suzukis gather at the 1987 Rhino Rally which was combined with the Off Road Show at Mansell Lacey. Below: Muddy progress for Rhino members at the 1987 event at Essex Arena.

trenches, sharply angled side crossings and breathtaking charges up hillsides so steep that all the driver – and passengers – can see through the windscreen is the sky above. It's terrain that stretches the off-road car's ability to its limits and tests the driver's skill as well; it's not just a matter of grabbing first gear and flooring the throttle.

At a Rhino Club event there will be experienced marshals on hand – usually enthusiast members of the All-Wheel Drive Club – who ensure that all participants understand the basics of off-road driving for their own safety, and that of their vehicles, and who offer free advice to anyone wishing to learn more about the finer techniques of controlling an all-terrain vehicle. The value of the Rhino Club's operation has been proved time and time again as ever more Suzuki owners flock to the meetings in search of genuine off-road action and excitement, in an enthusiastic environment, and with rescue services on hand to get anyone who does get stuck back into the swing of the day's events. Meetings are usually held over Bank Holiday weekends. Information on coming events should be available from any Suzuki dealer.

The Rhino Club provides a valuable service in allowing Suzuki owners to blow off cross-country steam under controlled conditions. It serves also, though, as a useful starting point for drivers wishing to vent their enthusiasm on more than the odd weekend occasion through the year. The best answer for such enthusiasts is to join the All-Wheel Drive Club. While this group has a hard core of Land Rover and Range Rover owners, ranks have been opened to four-wheel drive vehicles of all types and makes, again specifically to provide controlled off-road conditions where all-terrain cars may be driven to their full capabilities.

The All-Wheel Drive Club takes the standards of off-road driving to much higher levels than the Rhino Club. On offer are a wide range of events with non-damaging trials (this means it is very unlikely that the car's bodywork will suffer any damage in the course of the event) to senior trials (of such difficulty and over such tortuous terrain that damage could occur, even if only accidental removal of an exhaust system) and competition safaris, which equate to cross-country special-stage rallying. Membership of All-Wheel Drive Club (at time of writing) costs around £15 a year, with details available by writing to the club's headquarters in Aldershot, Hants, GU11 3BR.

Other possibilities exist, but only if you're prepared to travel. The Continentals are also enthusiastic off-roaders and British off-road club members are receiving more and more invitations to enter trials competitions in France and Germany.

The French are particularly keen on off-road driving, and they have more in the way of freely available rough terrain in which to vent their enthusiasm. The *Federation Sportive des Grands Randonneurs* – loosely translating as the Federation of Great Wanderers – organizes many regular annual events for off-road vehicles, including some exciting non-competitive tours. Several of their larger events might be of particular interest to Suzuki owners in Britain; though naturally dominated by French enthusiasts, in recent years the numbers of participants from other countries has grown – with the general enthusiasm for the sport of off-roading and outdoor living easily transcending any language barriers. In association with the petrol company Total, the *Grand Randonneurs* run winter and summer crossings of the Alps – the winter one involving much

The British Rhino Club Rally has become an important international event. These vehicles, including a door-less LJ80 right, and a long-wheelbase SJ with a hardtop, in front below, came from Holland for the 1987 event.

The Norwegian contingent at the 1987 Rhino Club Trial, below, and Team Norway's overall winner, Ole Geir Gjorvad, with his modified, big-wheeled SJ410.

The 1989 Rhino Rally at Long Valley near Aldershot attracted 131 entries for its trials events, won by Brian Snell's SJ.

Two entries in the graphics competition at the 1989 Rhino Rally. The charging rhino side panel is on Terry Friar's 'Brute Force' which gained the top graphics award. An SJ413 powered by a 125bhp Allard Turbo engine, this car claims 110mph maximum speed and 0–60mph in 7.5 sec!

ice and snow, calling for the use of tyre chains, winches and picks and shovels, is called the *Croisiere Blanche* (White Crossing), and the summer one, much easier because it's usually dry and dusty, is called The Hannibal, as it (more or less) follows Hannibal's trail across the Alps from France into Italy.

There's also an even called The Hexagonal; this is an allusion to the shape of the country of France, and involves an off-road dash all round the perimeter of the country. As with the Alpine crossings, this uses forestry tracks for much of its distance, though some difficult off-road stretches are included to keep up the excitement.

Tougher on cars and passengers – yet still well within the grasp of the Suzuki SJs – is the Aneto, a lengthways crossing of the Pyrenees from the Atlantic coast to the Mediterranean.

Wintry conditions for this RTV trial, with SJs and LJs lined up to take their turn over the special sections.

These events are not particularly expensive to enter, costing around £150-200 per vehicle. Participants are expected to make their own way to and from the event, which naturally puts up the cost for British enthusiasts having to add ferry fares, and they must feed themselves and camp out overnight. The atmosphere is always good, though, and since the events usually last around a week – in some cases two – they could form the basis of an enjoyable Continental holiday as well as providing a challenging outlet for the off-road driver's enthusiasm.

And, for the more adventurous, the same organization also runs three-week off-road safaris in the wilds of North Africa. For more information contact the *Grands Randonneurs'* headquarters at PO Box 1457, 30017 Nimes, France, or the Total Recreational Activities office at 84 Rue de Villiers, 92538 Levallois Perret, Paris.